Buffalo Bill Cody

Other titles in *Historical American Biographies*

Historical American Biographies

BUFFALO BILL CODY

Western Legend

Karen Bornemann Spies

Enslow Publishers, Inc.

44 Fadem Road
Box 699
Springfield, NJ 07081
USA

PO Box 38
Aldershot
Hants GU12 6BP
UK

Library of Congress Cataloging-in-Publication Data

Spies, Karen Bornemann.
    Buffalo Bill Cody: Western legend / Karen Bornemann Spies.
       p. cm. — (Historical American biographies)
    Includes bibliographical references (p.) and index.
    Summary: Traces the life of the legendary frontiersman, from his
childhood in the Kansas Territory, through his years of adventure as
military scout, Pony Express rider, and buffalo hunter, to his creation of
his Wild West Show.
    ISBN 0-7660-1015-5
    1. Buffalo Bill, 1846–1917—Juvenile literature. 2. Pioneers—West
(U.S.)—Biography—Juvenile literature. 3. Entertainers—United States—
Biography—Juvenile literature. 4. Buffalo Bill's Wild West Show—
History—Juvenile literature. 5. West (U.S.)—Biography—Juvenile
literature. [1. Buffalo Bill, 1846–1917. 2. West (U.S.)—Biography.]
I. Title. II. Series.
F594.B94S66 1998
978'.02'092—dc21
[B]   97-4357
                                         CIP
                                        AC

Printed in the United States of America

10 9 8 7 6 5 4 3 2

Illustration Credits: Buffalo Bill Memorial Museum, Lookout Mountain,
Colorado, City and County of Denver, Denver Mountain Parks, pp. 9,
13, 19, 22, 36, 56, 61, 63, 73; The Denver Public Library, Western
History Department, pp. 15, 33, 39, 44, 75, 87, 95, 102, 112; Stephen
Klimek, pp. 28, 48.

Cover Illustration: Corel Corporation (Background); Buffalo Bill
Memorial Museum, Lookout Mountain, Colorado, City and County of
Denver, Denver Mountain Parks (Inset).

CONTENTS

1

Showman of the Wild West

At the sound of the bugle, a tall, silver-haired man rode his prancing white stallion into the arena. His saddle sparkled with silver trim and the fringe on his beaded buckskin jacket swayed. With his thigh-high polished black boots, he appeared every inch the picture of a western hero.

Looking to the right and the left as he rode, he tipped his wide-brimmed cowboy hat to the crowd. "Ladies and Gentlemen," called out announcer Frank Richmond:

> I next have the honor of introducing to your attention a man whose record as a servant of the government,

whose skill and daring as a frontiersman, whose place
in history as the chief of scouts of the United States
Army . . . have made him well and popularly known
throughout the world . . . the Honorable William F.
Cody, "Buffalo Bill."[1]

For three decades, William F. Cody thrilled spectators with his Wild West show. It was the first and
the greatest of all the Wild West shows. In fact,
some writers consider it the greatest outdoor show
of all time.[2] Advertisements for the show called it
"America's National Entertainment, A Visit West in
Three Hours."[3]

Spectators could hardly wait to enter the
grandstands for each performance. The stands were
shaded with canvas awnings. They formed a
horseshoe around the rectangular, open-air arena. The
Cowboy Band signaled the start of the performance
by playing "The Star-Spangled Banner," which did not
become the official national anthem until 1931. Its
performance at outdoor entertainment or sporting
events was not yet customary.

Each show opened with the grand processional,
which Cody said showed the most colorful parts of
western life.[4] Act by act, the cast members entered
from behind a white canvas curtain stretched across
the end of the arena. Native Americans entered on
horseback, in war paint and feathers, followed by
vaqueros, Mexican cowboys, who galloped in waving
their sombreros. Six-foot-five-inch-tall Buck Taylor,

"King of the Cowboys," led the cowboys. Sheriff Con Groner looked impressive with his bowie knives, pistols, and rifle.

The Star of the Show

Last to enter was Buffalo Bill, William F. Cody, who rode in as a bugle called. He pulled up his white stallion in front of the main grandstand. "Ladies and Gentlemen," Cody announced. "Allow me to introduce the equestrian portion of the Wild West Exhibition." Turning to the waiting horseback riders, he asked, "Wild West, are you ready? Go!"[5]

From the very first act, the crowd never had a chance to get bored. The shows varied from year to

The Cowboy Band signaled the start of the show by playing "The Star-Spangled Banner."

year and new acts were added to keep interest high. Typically, the program began with a quarter-mile horse race. Next came the running of the Pony Express, presented at every performance in the history of the Wild West show. A rider dashed in and switched his mail pouch from one horse to another. His demonstration showed how letters were delivered across North America before the building of the transcontinental railroad and the telegraph. The spectators at the Wild West thrilled to the excitement of the fast-moving horses and the idea of riders racing against danger to deliver the mail.

After another race, the arena filled with cowboys and Native Americans re-creating perhaps the most famous battle of Cody's career as a scout. In 1876, he led part of the 5th Cavalry against a group of Cheyenne warriors. In a one-on-one fight, Cody killed and scalped a chief named Yellow Hair. Over the years, writers retold the story with more and more exaggeration.[6] It became a tale of a duel to the death between the two, with Yellow Hair challenging Cody by name. In the Wild West, the actor playing Yellow Hair called out to Cody, who galloped toward him on a stallion. As the two approached each other, they fired blanks. Then they fought in hand-to-hand combat until Cody "killed" and "scalped" Yellow Hair and the cowboys drove off the rest of the Native Americans.[7]

Real or Imaginary

Those who study Buffalo Bill's life sometimes have difficulty deciding which events are true and which are fictionalized. He arranged facts to suit his version of history. The battle with Yellow Hair is an example. Before the battle, Buffalo Bill expected the 5th Cavalry to fight Yellow Hair and the Cheyenne. Most likely, Cody knew he would later re-create this battle in his act.[8] He changed from his normal buckskin shirt and leggings into a show costume. It was a black velvet *vaquero*, or Mexican cowboy, outfit decorated in red, with silver buttons and lace trim. He did not usually wear a *vaquero* costume when scouting. But by wearing it in battle, Cody changed it from a mere costume to actual scouting clothing.[9] Cody had begun to combine western myth and real life.

Sharpshooting

Marksmanship came next on the show's bill. Seth Clover began by shooting at a glass ball tossed in the air. Next he shouldered his rifle, aimed, and shattered two glass balls thrown in the air at the same time. His shooting was so accurate that he also hit half-dollars, dimes, and nickels thrown into the air.

Johnny Baker, billed as the "Cowboy Kid," delighted audiences with his sharpshooting. Baker came from North Platte, Nebraska, where Buffalo Bill also had a home. The Cowboy Kid joined the

Wild West as a young boy. Buffalo Bill treated him like a son and taught him to shoot so well that Baker became a star of the Wild West. Baker shot his rifle from many positions such as leaning backward and over his head. He stood on his head and hit targets with his pistols.

The most popular Wild West performer, next to Buffalo Bill, was Annie Oakley. She could outshoot any of the men in the show. Billed as the "Little Girl of the Western Plains," Oakley had never been west of the Mississippi River until she became a show performer.[10] But that did not matter. She drew spectators to the show. Oakley could shoot an apple from the head of a trained dog. When a playing card was held edgewise, she sliced it in two with one shot. Oakley often finished her performance by shooting at glass balls with both her rifle and shotgun. Three glass balls were thrown in the air, one right after the other. She hit the first with the rifle held upside down upon her head. The next two she hit with her shotgun.

After that it was the cowboys' turn to put on a show, riding bucking horses and mules. This part of the show was called "Cowboy Fun." It finished with Buck Taylor riding at a full gallop and picking up his hat and handkerchief off the ground.

Next came the star of the show, the Honorable William F. Cody, Buffalo Bill, who was billed as "a practical all-around shot."[11] Cody used a .44 caliber,

Annie Oakley, known as "Little Sure Shot," could hit a target by looking in a mirror and balancing a rifle on her shoulder. She could slice a playing card in two with a single shot.

1873 model Winchester repeating rifle loaded with special, chilled shot pellets. Shot was safer to use than bullets, which might hit the spectators or nearby buildings.[12] After the performance of his first show, Buffalo Bill received a bill for the windows on a greenhouse eight blocks away that his bullets broke.[13]

Cody's act never failed to amaze his audiences. Shouldering his rifle, he rode full speed behind an assistant who tossed glass balls into the air. Buffalo Bill pointed his rifle high in the air at the balls, usually shattering them on his first try.[14]

Wild West Action!

"The Attack Upon the Deadwood Stage," an authentic stagecoach, always thrilled the crowd. Two to four passengers were picked from the audience to ride in the stagecoach. Shortly after the stagecoach rumbled off, the spectators heard a fierce yell. A group of Native Americans on horseback galloped after the stage. The driver turned his stagecoach and tried to flee. But the war party, continuing to whoop and shoot their rifles, followed closely. The courageous driver managed to keep his passengers safe until rescued by Cody and a group of cowboys.

Next audiences learned about Native American life, first observing a variety of dances. Sioux boys also raced bareback on ponies from one of Buffalo Bill's ranches.

Mustang Jack was a popular performer. Native Americans called him "Pets-ze-ca-we-cha-cha," the great high jumper.[15] He did a standing high jump of nearly six feet, which was higher than the world track-and-field record at that time. The crowd was delighted as he jumped over a variety of different-sized burros, ponies, and horses.

The show ended with "The Attack on a Settler's

Buffalo Bill displays his hunting technique in the Wild West arena. A variety of livestock appeared in the show including elk, deer, steers, and bears.

Cabin." A settler came home from the fields to have his supper. Quietly, a band of Native Americans sneaked up on his cabin and stole a horse. The settler's son spotted them and fired a warning shot. The father then rushed out of the cabin toward the approaching warriors. Just in time, the cowboys galloped in shooting and saved the cabin.

The entire cast then gathered in front of the grandstand for a "Final Salute" and Cody bid the audience good-bye. As the cast exited in a complicated figure-eight maneuver, the master of ceremonies thanked the crowd for their attention

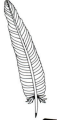

Life at the Show

What was life like for the Wild West cast? The show camp resembled a tent city. Performers lived in twelve-foot-square tents. Stars and owners had tents to themselves, while everyone else lived two to a tent. They went to the wardrobe tent for their costumes. The barber shop, laundry tent, and blacksmith shop were kept busy.

Performers were issued meal tickets, which they turned in at the door to the dining tent. The cast ate an enormous amount of food. A partial list of one week's menu included 5,694 pounds of beef, 350 pounds of bacon, 3,260 quarts of milk, 570 dozen eggs, and 500 pies.

and invited them to visit the Wild West camp.
Visitors were fascinated with the tents of the performers, especially those of the Native Americans
and stars such as Annie Oakley.

Cody, who was known for his friendliness, often
gave autographs to the children who came to the
show's back lots. He willingly posed when their
parents took photographs. He gave out free tickets
to orphans. His cousin, a social worker, asked about
bringing some of her needy charges to the show.
Cody responded in his typical way, "I love
children—bring them all."[16]

Circus showman P. T. Barnum said "Buffalo Bill is
known to more people by sight than any man living."[17] A newspaper reporter wrote that Cody's fame
and reputation were:

> well earned and merited. From the position of
> bull-whacker in the early days he passed through the
> various stations of wagon master, pony express rider,
> government scout, stock raiser, and actor until he
> stands today unrivaled as the greatest showman on the
> face of the earth.[18]

By entering show business, Cody became known
to people all over the world. More than any other
person, he built a romantic vision of the Old West
with his Wild West shows. His very nickname,
Buffalo Bill, painted a picture of a rugged hunter.
Cody lived a life full of adventure, and it began at a
very young age.

GROWING UP WITH ADVENTURE

Restless Isaac Cody always wanted to explore what was over the next hill or mountain. He moved west from Ohio to Scott County, Iowa, with his bride, Mary Ann Laycock. In 1840, they built a four-room log cabin, where their first child, Samuel, was born in 1841. In 1843, daughter Julia arrived, followed on February 26, 1846, by William Frederick Cody. Altogether, Isaac and Mary Ann Cody had eight children plus a daughter from Isaac's first marriage.

In 1847, the family moved again when Isaac Cody began managing a large farm for William F.

Brackenridge on Wapsipinicon River. Five years later, sadness struck. Twelve-year-old Samuel Cody rode out to the pasture to bring in the cows. His mare, Bettie, threw Samuel and rolled over on him. He died the next day from his injuries.

The family doctor ordered a change of scene for heartbroken Mary Ann Cody. Isaac had heard about new opportunities for settlers in Kansas. He decided it was time for a fresh start. Some of his father's need for elbow room had already rubbed off on William, nicknamed Willie or Will. He went with his father to Kansas to pick out their new homesite. Young Will Cody was thrilled by the sights and sounds at Fort Leavenworth, the first "real fort" he had seen.[1] He saw different Native American tribes and cavalrymen drilling with flashing swords. He was impressed with the men "dressed all in buckskin with coonskin caps or broad-brimmed slouch hats—real Westerners of whom I had dreamed."[2] The seeds of adventure were planted in Will's heart.

The Codys were one of the first families to move

Eighteen-month-old Will Cody lived in a log cabin near LeClaire in Scott County, Iowa.

to the Kansas Territory, where Isaac built a seven-room cabin. He planted crops and won a contract to supply hay and wood to Fort Leavenworth.

At age eight, Will got his first horse, a four-year-old pony he named Prince. Will's cousin, Horace Billings, was a circus performer who taught Prince to kneel and do tricks. Perhaps Will got some of his ideas for Wild West acts by watching Horace ride standing up on Prince's back.

A Dangerous Time

The peaceful situation in Kansas ended in May 1854, when Congress passed the Kansas-Nebraska Act. This law gave Kansas the right to choose to be either a free or slave state. Settlers hurried to stake their claims to land. Since some were proslavery and others antislavery, or abolitionists, bloody controversy lasted until Kansas became a free state in 1861.

Isaac Cody opposed the spread of slavery, but he was not an abolitionist. At a proslavery rally in September 1854, leaders challenged Isaac to speak. He repeated his opposition to the spread of slavery. Charles Dunn, a rally leader, was furious at Cody's comments. He stabbed Isaac in the back. Will, who was only eight years old, helped carry his father to safety at the nearby trading post.

Isaac's proslavery neighbors searched for him. When they failed to find him, they drove off his horses and burned his hay. They frightened Jennie Lyons, the teacher he had hired to instruct his and the neighboring children. When the proslavery supporters threatened to burn the schoolhouse, Miss Lyons resigned. Later, they stole Will's pony and threatened to blow up the Cody farmhouse.

His outspoken beliefs made it unsafe for Isaac to remain in Salt Creek, where the Codys lived. He left his family for a time and went to Grasshopper Falls to help antislavery families stake out homesite claims. Although his father returned home sometimes, Will took on more duties. He drove the family's two remaining cows out to pasture, fetched water from a nearby spring, and hunted for game. He rode into Leavenworth for supplies and the mail.

One day, Isaac's proslavery neighbors hid a short distance from the Cody home. They planned to ambush Isaac when he returned. Although Will was ill, he rode to Grasshopper Falls to warn his father. Father and son returned home unharmed nearly two weeks later. While resting at home, Isaac hid in a cornfield, hoping to avoid the proslavery people. He wore a dress, sun bonnet, and cape so he would look like a woman from a distance.

Although he recovered from his stab wound, Isaac never fully regained his health. He caught a chill helping settlers from Cleveland, Ohio, move into Grasshopper Falls. His chill turned into pneumonia, and Isaac died on March 10, 1857. The Cody family, however, felt the stabbing was the true cause of Isaac's death.[3]

Will Cody Goes to Work

Isaac's death left the Codys needing money. Mary Ann rented out the farm and sold the horses. Eleven-year-old Will drove an ox team to Leavenworth for fifty cents a day. After that job, he worked as a messenger for the freight firm of Russell, Majors, and Waddell. Riding his mule, Will delivered messages between the company store and the tele-graph office at Fort Leavenworth. He soon found the job boring because there was not enough rid-ing and too much sitting.[4] Trail boss John Willis then hired Will to herd his oxen. Will liked this job

and proudly wore the revolver Willis gave him.

By the age of twelve, Will had already learned many outdoor skills. He could hunt, fish, and handle horses and oxen. But he had not

At age twelve, Will helped support the Cody family. He hunted, tended crops, and had worked on a wagon train.

attended school for three years. In the summer of 1857, Mary Ann Cody took in a boarder who had been a teacher in Illinois. He taught Will, along with around fifteen other students. Will met his first girl-friend, Mary Hyatt, during this time. Will built her a playhouse in the schoolyard, hoping to impress her. An older boy, Stephen Gobel, knocked it down, so Will fought back. Stephen pinned Will to a wall. Will pulled out his pocketknife and cut Stephen's thigh. Stephen cried to the teacher that Will had tried to kill him.[5]

The sheriff and Stephen's father came looking for Will in trail boss John Willis's yard, so Will hid in one of Willis's wagons. The trail boss did not give away his hiding place. Later, he brought Will home and asked Mary Ann Cody for permission to take Will on a month-long trip to Fort Kearny. "The trip was a most enjoyable one for me," Will wrote, "although no incidents worthy of note occurred on the way."[6]

Frontier Adventures

According to legend, it was during this time that Will shot his first Native American. Some writers give his age as eleven, while others believe he was twelve or thirteen.[7] He was on a cattle drive when Native Americans stampeded the herd, killing three herders. The trail bosses regrouped the men and started back toward Fort Kearny, Nebraska. Cody wrote later that he saw a Native American peering over the creek bank. "Instead of hurrying ahead and alarming the men in a quiet way," he said, "I instantly aimed my gun at the head and fired."[8] The herders drove off the rest of the warriors.

Cody lived at a time when such events were not unusual. As white settlers moved into the frontier, they pushed out the Native Americans who had been living there. Cavalry soldiers, wagon train leaders, scouts, and other whites living on the frontier did kill Native Americans, at times in self-defense. Unfortunately, on other occasions, they attacked the Native Americans. Any killing Cody did was in self-defense or as part of his job as a guide and a scout. As an adult, Cody said that he regretted any killing he had done.[9] He believed that in the majority of disputes between whites and Native Americans, "it will be found that the white man is responsible for the dispute through breaking faith with them."[10]

Will's next adventure came while working on one of Lewis Simpson's wagon trains in 1857. Twenty-five wagons lumbered along, each carrying six thousand pounds of freight. On this trip, Will met Wild Bill Hickok. When Hickok defended him against a bully, Will considered the scout a close friend for life.[11]

One day, a group of Mormons ambushed the wagon train. Mormons belong to a religious faith known as the Church of Jesus Christ of Latter-Day Saints. They played an important role in settling the West by founding Salt Lake City and helping to create the state of Utah.[12] Over the years, the Mormons had been driven out of their homes by other settlers who were frightened of their religious views. President James Buchanan sent Army troops to stop the fighting between Mormons and those opposed to them. The Mormons sometimes attacked wagon trains such as Simpson's to prevent supplies from reaching the troops.

The Mormon ambush left Simpson and his crew with just enough supplies to fill one wagon. Will's exciting wagon train job became a plodding journey on foot. It took the crew about a month to reach Fort Bridger in the Nebraska Territory (later Wyoming), where they spent the winter.

When he returned home from the trip, Will's dog Turk recognized him, but his family might not have. Will's hair was a long, matted mess filled with bugs. His mother and sisters made him cut and wash it and take a bath before he could enter the house. They took his dirty clothes and burned them.

In the summer and fall of 1858, Will worked on wagon trains. He spent some time at Fort Laramie in the Nebraska Territory, where he saw Kit Carson,

Jim Bridger, and other famous scouts. He sat for hours watching Carson and other scouts "talk to the Indians in sign language. Without a sound they would carry on long and interesting conversations, tell stories, inquire about game and trails."[13] By playing with the Native American children in the villages there, he began learning sign language. It became a foundation for his future as a scout.

In January 1859, Will returned to Salt Creek, Kansas. He had had many exciting adventures, but he still could not read or write well. Will spent the next two and a half months in school, the longest period of schooling he ever had. He improved his reading and writing but never became very good at spelling or math. His education ended in the late spring of 1859 when gold was discovered in Colorado. He joined the rush but did not strike it rich.

The Pony Express

At age fourteen or fifteen, Will took on the challenge of riding for the Pony Express.[14] He started on the forty-five-mile stretch that began in Julesburg, Colorado. A few months later, he rode a longer route, seventy-six miles from Red Buttes to Three Crossings, Wyoming Territory. One day, Will made an even longer ride. When he reached Three Crossings, he found that his relief rider had been killed in a brawl. Will then climbed onto a fresh mount and galloped toward the next station, Rocky Ridge, where he grabbed the mailbag bound for the East. He then headed back to Red Buttes, where he had started. The entire trip totaled 322 miles, one of the longest rides in Pony Express history. Cody later wrote that it took him twenty-one hours and forty minutes and that he used twenty-one horses.[15]

Danger became a fact of life for Pony Express riders. In his autobiography, Cody wrote about his run from Horse Creek Station toward Sweetwater Bridge in Wyoming Territory. During his ride, fifteen Native

The Pony Express

After the discovery of gold in California in 1848, thousands of people moved west. Letters sent by steamship or stagecoach were slow to arrive. On April 3, 1860, William Russell, Alexander Majors, and William Waddell started a new, faster mail company using a network of riders on horseback. It was called the Pony Express.

Riders were paid to cover fifteen miles each hour in a system Cody later called "a relay race against time."[16] Each rider's route covered three stations, and he changed horses at each one. Messages were carried in a waterproof leather saddlebag known as a *mochila*. As the rider galloped into the station, he yanked the *mochila* out from under him. He leaped off his mount, tossed the saddlebag onto the saddle horn of a waiting horse, and raced off again.

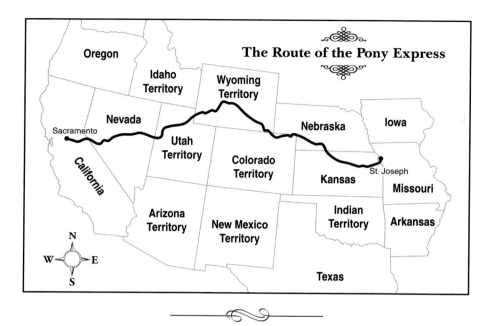

The Pony Express carried mail between St. Joseph, Missouri, and Sacramento, California. Will Cody was a rider on the Wyoming Territory section of the route.

Americans attacked. He stayed ahead of them with his fast riding. When he rode into the station at Sweetwater Bridge, however, no fresh mount waited in the corral. Native Americans had killed the station master and driven off all the horses. Will rode on and arrived safely at Plant's Station, twelve miles away.[17]

When Cody began his Wild West show years later, he used the Pony Express and many of his other early experiences to create popular acts. He lived a life of adventure. Perhaps that is why he, like his father, had trouble staying in one place and settling down.

A WAR AND
A WEDDING

Today many of Buffalo Bill Cody's adventures seem fantastic, because that is how they have been portrayed by television, books, and movies. Some might even consider Cody a juvenile delinquent. As a boy, he slashed another young man with a knife and killed a Native American. During the Civil War, he started out as a horse thief.[1] In April 1861, when the war began, Cody was fifteen. He could have enlisted as a drummer boy, but his mother was ill with tuberculosis, a lung disease known at the time as consumption. She made him promise that he would not enlist in a regular Army unit while she was alive.

Instead, Cody joined a private army. Kansas was a free state, but many people in Missouri, the next state to the east, supported slavery. Cody had strong antislavery beliefs, especially since he felt proslavery people had caused his father's death. He met a man named Chandler who suggested they form an independent group "for the purpose of invading Missouri and making war on its people our own responsibility."[2] In bands of two or three, they raided the farms of those known to be proslavery. They took their horses, which Cody admitted "may look to the reader like horse-stealing."[3] The group claimed the raids were legal, because they were an act of war against a proslavery, Southern state. As Cody said, "we didn't let our consciences trouble us very much."[4]

When Mary Ann Cody learned about Chandler's group, she ordered her son to quit. She insisted that their actions were illegal and dishonorable. Detectives had arrested several of the raiders. Cody went along with his mother's request, admitting that his actions truly were illegal.

For the next two years, Cody worked for wagon train companies, carried military dispatches, and did some scouting. He was with an Army wagon train in Denver, Colorado, in the fall of 1863 when he received news that his mother was dying. He arrived home before she died on November 22. Cody was

Jayhawkers

When Congress passed the Kansas-Nebraska Act in 1854, battles between proslavery and free-state groups broke out. Soon the territory was called "Bleeding Kansas." Proslavery armed bands from Missouri, called bushwhackers, attacked free-state settlers. The free-state settlers, who formed groups of their own, became known as jayhawkers.

During the Civil War, the name jayhawker applied to anyone in a private antislavery army such as the one William F. Cody joined. Unfortunately, many of these men committed terrible crimes, like setting fire to homes of people who favored slavery or murdering those who disagreed with them. The term jayhawker became a negative one meaning "thief."[5] Cody did not commit murder or any other crimes when he served with his free-state group. However, proslavery advocates called him a jayhawker, meaning it in a critical way.

Today, the term is used in a positive fashion. Jayhawker is a nickname for a resident of Kansas.

greatly saddened by the loss. He later wrote, "I loved her above all other persons."[6]

A Regular Army Man

Cody found his home so gloomy without his mother that he fled to Leavenworth, Kansas. For about two months, he kept company with gamblers and drunkards. Then the 7th Kansas Volunteer Cavalry of the United States Army returned. On February 19,

1864, Cody enlisted in the group. Later he claimed that his joining up was the result of drinking too much bad whiskey, since he could not remember how he had come to sign up.[7] Whatever his reason for joining, he was determined to make a success of his stint in the Army.

By this time, he was eighteen years old. Official records show he was five feet ten inches tall with brown eyes and brown hair.[8] He served in the Army for over a year and a half. His regiment fought several important battles in Mississippi and Tennessee and helped defend the city of St. Louis, Missouri.

A favorite story of Cody's described one of his experiences as an Army scout and spy. Dressed in Confederate gray, Cody stopped at a farmhouse behind rebel lines. Another man was already there, eating bread and milk. The man was Wild Bill Hickok, disguised as a Confederate officer. As the story goes, he secretly gave Cody important reports to take north.[9]

Toward the end of the war, Cody served as a hospital orderly in St. Louis. An orderly performs everyday tasks such as carrying messages and moving supplies. In St. Louis, he made a crucial decision. On May 1, 1865, he met a dark-eyed young woman named Louisa Frederici. Her cousin William McDonald, a friend and fellow soldier of Cody's, brought Cody to her home for a visit.[10] She was

Famous western hero Wild Bill Hickok is dressed in typical scouting attire. He befriended young Will Cody on a wagon train trip.

reading a book when suddenly the chair was pulled out from under her. Louisa thought her cousin had played this trick on her, so she turned to slap him. The man she actually hit was Will Cody. Louisa blushed from embarrassment and apologized when introduced to Cody. They began dating that night.

Cody wrote that he greatly admired Louisa and spent many pleasant hours in her company.[11] He had never before met an educated, proper young lady, and he felt she had a gentle disposition and graceful manners.[12] Louisa found Cody equally impressive.[13] She considered him the most handsome man she had ever met.

Life After the War

After Cody's Army discharge as a private on September 29, 1865, scouting took up much of his time. He worked for William Tecumseh Sherman, a Union general of the Civil War. Sherman was in charge of a group of peace commissioners who were traveling from Fort Zarah to Council Springs (now Wichita, Kansas) to meet with the Kiowa and Comanches. Chief guide Dick Curtis was leading the party too far west. Cody impressed Sherman by assuming the lead and guiding the group straight to Council Springs.

Soon after, Cody drove a stagecoach for Ben Holliday's Overland Stage Line. Holliday's idea of a stagecoach driver's outfit was a broad-brimmed sombrero, corduroy pants trimmed with velvet, and high-heeled boots. Each driver proudly snapped a nine-foot rawhide whip with a glinting silver handle. Perhaps these costumes later inspired those in Cody's Wild West show. In any case, Cody became one of the showiest, fastest drivers with his team of four gray horses.[14]

After his stint as a stagecoach driver, Cody returned to St. Louis, where he and Louisa were married on March 6, 1866. Unfortunately, Louisa would probably have been better off marrying someone else. She wanted a stay-at-home life, while Cody wanted adventure. She loved the East, and he admired the West. Louisa especially disliked show business. As a result, they spent more time apart than together. Some historians feel that during his entire married life, Cody did not stay at home for more than six consecutive months at any one time.[15] However, he became a loving father and did try to be a good husband. He affectionately nicknamed his wife "Lulu."

Cody and Louisa's honeymoon set the tone for their marriage. After the wedding ceremony, they boarded a riverboat bound for Leavenworth. Horsemen galloped up, threatening to shoot Cody for his antislavery views.[16] Louisa fainted as deck hands pulled away the gangplank, but the riverboat was

After the Civil War ended, Cody married Louisa Frederici. They soon found out that they had different ideas about marriage. She wanted a stay-at-home life, and he wanted adventure.

safely underway. A more friendly group greeted them at the dock at Leavenworth, Kansas. Officers from the fort and a brass band met them, and they had a reception at the home of Cody's sister Eliza. Louisa later wrote that the "cultured men and cultured women" she met at the fort and the dances they put on gave her a positive first impression of Kansas.[17]

Cody's first attempt at settling down involved renting the house his mother had once owned in Salt Creek Valley. He and Louisa planned to run it as a hotel. Unfortunately, Cody became an overly generous host and began to lose too much money. As his sister Helen put it, "travelers without money . . . would go miles out of their way to put up at his tavern."[18] After six months, he gave up on the hotel. Cody felt he could make more money in the West.

Thus began his first separation from his wife. Louisa stayed in Leavenworth, where their first child, a daughter named Arta, was born on December 16, 1866. Cody came home to see the baby and help choose her name. Then he was off again, this time to Fort Ellsworth, Kansas.

Leaving the hotel business represented a turning point in Cody's life. If he had stayed at home, living the life of a settler, he probably would not have become Buffalo Bill Cody or started his Wild West shows.

4

SCOUTING
AND
HUNTING

Cody rode west to Junction City, Kansas. There he ran into Wild Bill Hickok, who was working as a scout at Fort Ellsworth, Kansas. Cody signed up for the same job. Much of his fame today comes from his activities as a scout. He began by guiding General George Armstrong Custer south from Fort Hays, Kansas, to Fort Larned, Kansas. Custer was so impressed with Cody's guiding skills that he offered Cody a scouting job any time he was available.[1]

On August 2, 1867, Cody fought in his first large battle with Native Americans. Thirty-four soldiers faced three hundred warriors. The troops came from Company F, 10th United States Cavalry, a new

Cody earned fame and respect as a scout for the Army. He was an excellent marksman with great courage and endurance.

regiment made up of African-American soldiers. Cody guided the regiment back to Fort Hays with only one soldier killed and one wounded.

Soon after this battle, Cody teamed up with William Rose, who had a contract to grade, or level and smooth, the railroad beds near Fort Hays for the Kansas Pacific Railroad. The two men planned to make their fortunes by forming a new town near where the railroad would pass just west of the fort. They named the town Rome and gave free lots to anyone who would build on them. Cody and Rose purchased supplies and opened a store. Cody sent for Louisa and Arta, who would live in the rear of the store. According to Cody, within a month, Rome contained two hundred homes, three or four stores, a hotel, and several saloons.[2]

But Rome was doomed to failure. Dr. William Webb, a railroad agent, asked to join the partners, but they refused. So Webb founded his own town nearby, calling it Hays City. He spread the word that the railroad would build a machine shop and roundhouse there. (A roundhouse is a building where locomotives are stored and repaired.) Believing the roundhouse and machine shop would make Hays City a bustling center of business, most of Rome's residents moved there. With Rome nearly empty, Louisa took Arta back to St. Louis, leaving her husband free to decide what to do next with his life.

Earning a Famous Nickname

His next step helped to earn him the legendary nickname "Buffalo Bill."[3] While grading the roadbed for the railroad, he hitched his horse, Brigham, to a heavy scraper. The work went slowly, because Brigham was not a powerful workhorse. He was, however, a speedy buffalo hunter. Brigham was so good that if the buffalo did not fall at the first shot, he stopped and gave Cody a second chance.[4] If that shot missed, Brigham went on to the next buffalo in the herd.

One day, Cody spotted an approaching herd of buffalo. He unhitched Brigham from the scraper, grabbed his rifle, and rode bareback after the small herd. Also in pursuit were a group of Army officers led by Captain George W. Graham. Cody wrote that the officers laughed and said he and Brigham would not be able to keep up.[5] They promised to share their buffalo meat with Cody.

The herd ran toward a nearby creek. Cody knew that once buffalo ran toward water, they rarely changed course. He steered Brigham toward the creek. When the buffalo stampeded past, Brigham responded. With a few jumps, he brought Cody alongside the last buffalo in the herd. Cody dropped the animal with one shot. Brigham then brought him alongside the next buffalo. One by one, Cody shot eleven buffalo with twelve shots. The Army officers

The Destruction of the Buffalo

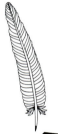

Because of his famous nickname, Buffalo Bill is often blamed for the elimination of the buffalo herds. This claim is not supported by facts. During his lifetime, Cody killed, at the most, ten thousand buffalo. The majority of these he killed only for food.[6] The slaughter of the buffalo really began in the 1870s, when white hunters discovered how Europeans prized the fine leather of buffalo hides, and began to kill only for the hide. Historians estimate that from 1872 to 1874, an average of five thousand buffalo were killed each day.[7] This widespread killing began after Cody had quit his buffalo-hunting job. In fact, the Smithsonian Institution issued a report in 1887 that credited Buffalo Bill with helping to restore the buffalo by keeping herds in both his Wild West show and on his ranches.

did not bag a single buffalo, so Cody shared his meat with them. Captain Graham quickly told others about Cody's skill, calling him "Buffalo Bill."[8]

Railroad workmen soon began to use the nickname. In October 1867, Cody signed a contract with the Kansas Pacific to supply at least twelve buffalo a day to feed the workers. The possibility of Native American attacks and the skills required to be a buffalo hunter made the job a high-paying one. He earned $500 a month, a large wage for that time.[9] A private in the frontier army was paid just

$13 a month. During the eighteen months he was on the railroad's payroll, Cody claimed he killed 4,280 buffalo.[10] The true figure is probably closer to three thousand, since he actually hunted for only eight months.

Sometimes, Cody felt the workers may not have meant his nickname in a complimentary way. Tired of eating buffalo meat every day, they sang this jingle whenever they saw him:

Buffalo Bill, Buffalo Bill
Never missed and never will.
Always aims and shoots to kill
And the company pays his buffalo bill.[11]

Many western history writers claim that author Ned Buntline gave Cody his nickname.[12] Buntline's real name was Edward Zane Carroll Judson. He went to sea as a young boy and took the nickname "buntline" from the rope at the bottom of a square sail. He first used the name to hide his identity when he wrote a story that was critical of his sea captain. As an adult, Buntline continued his career as an author.

As legend has it, Buntline went west in 1869, looking for ideas for adventure stories. He particularly wanted to meet Major Frank North, a hero in the Battle of Summit Springs.[13] North did not want to talk about his adventures. However, he did point out a young man sleeping under a wagon

BEADLE'S

Dime
New York
Library

10

Copyrighted, 1895, by BEADLE AND ADAMS.   ENTERED AS SECOND CLASS MATTER AT THE NEW YORK, N. Y., POST OFFICE.   February 13, 1895.

No. 851.   Published Every Wednesday.   Beadle & Adams, Publishers,   Ten Cents a Copy. $5.00 a Year.   Vol. LXVI.
95 WILLIAM STREET, NEW YORK.

BUFFALO BILL'S DOUBLE DILEMMA

OR, THE

Great Scout's Big Three

A ROMANCE OF

THE PONY RIDERS of the OVERLAND.

BY COL. PRENTISS INGRAHAM,
AUTHOR OF "BUFFALO BILL" NOVELS, ETC.

CHAPTER I.

THE MYSTERIOUS WARNING.

"If Buffalo Bill had not just made a double run because Jess Jordan was killed, he'd make the ride, boys."

"Well, plucky as I admit Buffalo Bill is—

Dime novels pictured Buffalo Bill as a legendary superhero. The public loved these inexpensive, fantastic stories. Hundreds of original dime novels were written about Buffalo Bill.

and suggested that Buntline interview him. That young man was William F. Cody. After their meeting, Buntline wrote *Buffalo Bill, the King of Border Men*. It was the first of hundreds of dime novels written about Buffalo Bill.

Did Buntline give Cody his nickname, as many writers suggest? Did the Buntline books about Buffalo Bill make Cody and his nickname famous? The facts do not support these statements.[14] Buntline wrote only four Buffalo Bill novels. Buntline's real claim to promoting Buffalo Bill's fame was that he introduced Cody to the theater and the idea of performing onstage.

Chief of Scouts

In 1868, Louisa and baby Arta returned from St. Louis to live with Cody in Hays, Kansas, until May, when the Kansas Pacific Railroad finished laying tracks. The railroad no longer needed Cody's services as a buffalo hunter. He sold his buffalo horse, Brigham, and signed on as a scout with the 10th Cavalry at Fort Hays, Kansas. Louisa and Arta went back to Leavenworth, Kansas, to live.

In August, Cody volunteered for an especially dangerous mission through Native American territory, carrying messages from one fort to another. The ride earned Cody the deep respect of General Philip Sheridan. He hired Cody as chief of scouts for the 5th Cavalry. During the next year, Cody served in seven expeditions and nine battles against the Native Americans. No other Army scout built as strong a record.

In May 1869, the 5th Cavalry was sent to Fort McPherson, Nebraska, where Cody and his family stayed until December 1872. While there, he worked with Brevet Major General Eugene A. Carr, who called him a "wonderful shot, tracker, and scout."[15] By this time, Cody was so famous for his scouting skills that the government awarded him a bonus of one hundred dollars, which had never been done before.

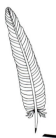

Scouting Around

The job of scouting carried great importance on the frontier.[16] Scouts marked trails and led settlers and soldiers westward. By studying the ground, trees, and bushes, they located food and clean water for settlers and found clues that saved troops and wagon trains from Native American attacks. On other occasions, they carried messages from one Army fort to another. These scouts were expected to fight as soldiers. Many scouts, including Buffalo Bill, received the Congressional Medal of Honor for their service.

In July 1869, the Cheyenne chief Tall Bull took his Dog Soldiers on the warpath. The Dog Soldiers were a fierce, military-like group within the larger Cheyenne tribe. Cody led Carr and his troops straight to the Cheyenne camp. On July 11, the 5th Cavalry defeated the Dog Soldiers and won what became known as the Battle of Summit Springs (in present-day Colorado). This victory opened western Kansas and southwestern Nebraska to settlement by whites. During the fighting, Cody shot Tall Bull and captured his horse, which he named Tall Bull.

On November 26, 1870, Cody's second child and only son was born at Fort McPherson, Nebraska. His parents named him Kit Carson Cody after Cody's friend and scouting companion. They nicknamed him "Kitty."

Cody's skill as a scout and buffalo hunter brought him to the attention of rich and famous men who wanted him to lead hunting parties. In September 1871, he led a hunt that many historians feel gave him the ideas that led to the development of the Wild West shows.[17] General Sheridan brought in friends from New York for ten days of hunting. According to General Henry Davies, a member of the group, Cody looked "to perfection the bold hunter and gallant sportsman of the prairies."[18]

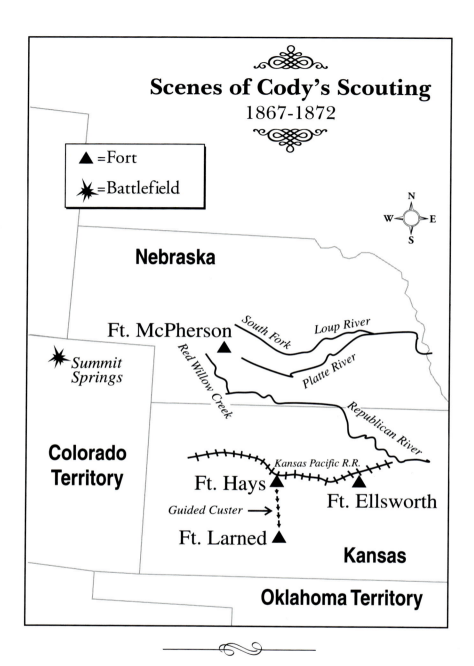

Scenes of Cody's Scouting
1867-1872

▲ =Fort

✴ =Battlefield

N W E S

Nebraska

Ft. McPherson

South Fork

Loup River

Red Willow Creek

✴ *Summit Springs*

Platte River

Colorado Territory

Republican River

Kansas Pacific R.R.

Ft. Hays ▲

Ft. Ellsworth ▲

Guided Custer →

Ft. Larned ▲

Kansas

Oklahoma Territory

Cody won fame and respect as chief of scouts for the 5th Cavalry. This map shows some of the places Cody worked during his years as a scout.

Hunting with the Grand Duke

In January 1872, Cody led his most famous hunt for Grand Duke Alexis, son of Czar Alexander II of Russia. Because it was conducted on such a grand scale, the hunt caught the interest of Americans and earned Buffalo Bill a huge amount of publicity.[19] General Sheridan sent two of his assistants to Fort McPherson, Nebraska, to prepare for the arrival of the royal party. Cody suggested they set up "Camp Alexis" near Red Willow Creek, forty miles south of the fort. They brought in tents with carpeted floors, comfortable furniture, and heating stoves. Camp Alexis was certainly not "roughing it." To add excitement, Cody asked Sioux leader Spotted Tail to take part in the hunt with one hundred of his warriors.

On January 13, the grand duke arrived on a special train. The hunt began the next morning at about nine o' clock. The duke, by agreement of the rest of the group, would get the first chance to shoot a buffalo. He rode Buffalo Bill's best horse, Buckskin Joe. Cody later wrote that the duke fired six shots wildly, missing with all of them.[20] Cody traded pistols with the duke. The next six shots missed their mark as well. Cody then gave Alexis his rifle. He told him to urge Buckskin Joe close to the buffalo and listen for Cody's signal to shoot. This time the grand duke hit a buffalo, and the entire hunting party cheered.

That night, they enjoyed a sumptuous dinner. It began with buffalo tail soup, followed by broiled fish, stewed rabbit, and buffalo with mushrooms. Next came roast elk, antelope chops, deer, and wild turkey. Side dishes included mashed potatoes and green peas. For dessert, if anyone had room, there was tapioca pudding.[21]

In five days of hunting, the grand duke hit eight buffalo. On the way back to his railroad car, the duke rode with General Sheridan and Buffalo Bill in an open carriage. When he learned that Cody had once been a stagecoach driver, Alexis asked him to take over the driving. Cody let the horses have more rein than he had planned. "Every once in a while," he wrote, "the hind wheels would strike a rut and take a bound, and not touch the ground again for fifteen or twenty feet."[22] After the wild ride, they arrived safely at the duke's train. Alexis had enjoyed the hunt so thoroughly that he gave Cody a Russian fur robe and a stickpin and diamond-studded cuff links shaped like buffalo heads.

Winning a Medal

In 1872, Cody received the Congressional Medal of Honor for his bravery in battle as a scout for Company B, 3rd Cavalry, from Fort McPherson, Nebraska. The troops were in pursuit of a Sioux war party that had killed two or three white men about five miles from the fort. On April 26, Cody guided a patrol of six soldiers to within fifty yards of the warriors, who were camped beside a creek that branched off the South Fork of the Loup River. The Native Americans opened fire. Cody's sharp aim killed one Sioux and Army troopers killed two others. The remaining warriors tried to escape, running for their horses, which were on the other side of the creek. The soldiers tried to follow on horseback, but only Cody's Buckskin Joe would jump the creek. Cody kept up with the chase, killing two more warriors. Captain Charles Meinhold, Cody's commanding officer, praised the scout for his brave actions.

The government later took away Cody's Medal of Honor. This medal, the highest award given by the United States, is supposed to be awarded only to members of the armed services. As a scout, Cody was a civilian. An act of Congress on June 16, 1916, struck his name from the records. However, in 1989, Congress restored the names of Cody and four other civilian scouts to the Medal of Honor Roll.

On August 15, 1872, the Codys' third child, Orra Maude, was born at Fort McPherson, Nebraska. Soon after her birth, Buffalo Bill's friends put his name on the ballot for the Nebraska legislature. Probably because of his fame, he was elected, but by only forty-four votes. Cody, proud of his victory, wrote, "That is the way in which I acquired my title of Honorable."[23] His political career turned out to be a short one. Some ballots had been sent to the wrong location for counting. A recount gave the victory to Cody's opponent.

Cody's loss was history's gain. He was about to embark on a new venture that would make his name famous in households across North America and Europe.

5

BECOMING A STAR

In 1872, General Sheridan gave Cody a leave of absence from scouting. He hopped on the eastbound train to Chicago and New York. In New York, Ned Buntline took Cody to see the play that had been made from Buntline's book *Buffalo Bill, the King of Border Men*. The spectators clapped loudly when they learned that the real Buffalo Bill was in the audience. They wanted him to go up on stage, but the brave scout suddenly found himself frightened. Buntline offered him five hundred dollars per week, a vast sum in those days, if he would play himself in the show. Cody refused, saying, "It would be useless for me to attempt anything of the kind, for I never could talk to a crowd of people like that, even if it was to save my neck, and that he [Buntline] might as well try to make an actor of a government mule."[1] However, within a few months, Cody changed his mind about appearing on stage.

After his visit to the East, Cody went back to scouting. In the summer of 1872, Buntline convinced both Cody and fellow scout Texas Jack Omohundro to try acting in his plays. The decision was tough, because Cody loved his life as a scout. But he told his wife, "I don't know just how bad I'd be at actin'. I guess maybe I'd better find out."[2]

On December 16, 1872, *The Scouts of the Prairie* opened to a packed theater. As soon as he stepped on stage, Cody forgot his lines. Buntline, realizing that Cody had stage fright, asked him about his life on the plains. Cody answered, totally at ease. He never spoke a word of his part, but the public did not mind. According to the *Chicago Tribune*, they were "too busy admiring Buffalo Bill in his buckskin shirt and leggings and fairly bristling with revolvers, knives, and rifles."[3] A *New York Herald* reporter wrote, "Everything is so wonderfully bad it is almost good."[4]

The play was extremely popular. In Boston, the production earned $16,200 in one week alone.[5] When the season ended on June 16, 1873, Cody was disappointed because Buntline paid him only six thousand dollars for his efforts. Texas Jack also felt that Buntline had not been fair in the financial dealings with him and Cody.[6] Buntline could not reach an agreement with Texas Jack and Buffalo Bill to do future performances. Cody then realized he could branch out on his own. With a good play, audiences might make him rich.[7] Cody and Texas Jack decided to form their own theater company for the next season. Buffalo Bill was not yet much of an actor, but he already loved the crowd's applause. He had begun to realize that he was a true showman.

His Own Theater Company

Cody's life now took a new direction. Every fall through spring, he toured with the Buffalo Bill Combination, the traveling theater group that he and Texas Jack formed. They usually presented one play, but sometimes the Combination sold enough tickets for two performances in one city. In that case, a different drama was presented at the second performance. In the summer, Cody continued to scout. This kept his frontiersman image alive.

In 1873, Cody and Texas Jack cut short their scouting to return east. Cody had purchased a home in Rochester, New York. Texas Jack also put down roots there. On August 31, Texas Jack married Giuseppina Morlacchi, the female star of *The Scouts*

Wild Bill Hickok, Texas Jack Omohundro, and Buffalo Bill (left to right) posed for a photograph to advertise one of their plays.

of the Prairie. Her manager, Major John M. Burke, became a member of the Buffalo Bill Combination. He remained with Cody for forty years as a publicity agent, faithfully building Buffalo Bill's legend.

The partners developed a new play, similar to that of the previous year, even down to its title, *The Scouts of the Plains*. However, new actors joined Cody and Texas Jack. White men, called "supers," played the parts of Native Americans. Wild Bill Hickok took Ned Buntline's place as co-star. Though he seemed like the ideal replacement, Hickok caused problems for the show. He could not get along well with the other cast members and refused to follow the script.[8] He threw his pistol at a spotlight because the glare bothered his eyes. He also shot blanks at the legs of the supers, which caused powder burns. The supers hopped wildly from foot to foot, trying to avoid the painful burns. Cody asked Hickok to stop doing this or leave the show. Hickok left.

During the summer of 1875, Cody went home to Rochester, where Louisa had been staying with the children while the Combination toured. This may have been the only summer he ever spent quietly at home with his family.[9]

Legendary Author

Buffalo Bill was fast becoming a legend. Stories of his deeds appeared in wildly exaggerated form in

The Dime Novel

Dime novels made popular reading from about the time of the Civil War to the turn of the century. They cost ten cents and were approximately sixty thousand words long. "Half-dime" novels contained about thirty thousand words and cost only five cents. Dime novels were similar to today's comic books, but without the pictures. They usually came out weekly. Each contained a thrilling story filled with action. Although some were detective or crime stories, the most popular described frontier adventure.

The Buffalo Bill dime novels contained exciting stories where the hero, Buffalo Bill, faced danger and always made the right choice. Usually, he performed bravely in battle or rescued someone, often a young woman. These stories exaggerated his talents to the point that he became a superhero. Parents sometimes complained that the fantastic stories lured eastern boys to the West. Yet reading these fanciful stories provided hours of enjoyment, and helped build Buffalo Bill's legendary image.

books called dime novels. On August 9, 1875, *The Pearl of the Prairies; or, The Scout and the Renegade* appeared. Experts believe it was the first of the twenty-two novels Cody may have written.[10] He also penned plays, short stories, essays, and autobiographies. Historians have preserved one manuscript in his own handwriting. *Grand Duke*

Alexis Buffalo Hunt, a novel, contains Cody's typical misspellings and lack of punctuation. As he told his sister Helen, "Life is too short to make big letters when small ones will do; and as for punctuation, if my readers don't know enough to take their breath without those little marks, they'll have to lose it, that's all."[11] In 1879, author Prentiss Ingraham probably took over writing the dime novels signed by Buffalo Bill.[12] He wrote 121 books, nine of them in 1892 alone.[13] He and other authors wrote a total of 557 different dime novels about Buffalo Bill. Countless additional translations and reprints appeared in Europe. They all helped build the picture of Buffalo Bill as a legendary hero and created the myth of western frontier life.

Developing as an Actor

For the 1875–1876 season, the Combination again performed in *The Scouts of the Plains.* The reputation of the company had improved, and Cody had earned respect as a character actor. Little by little, Cody developed a new kind of performance with western features.[14] The Combination hired actors who could also perform in shooting and roping exhibitions between the acts of the play. Some critics were disappointed that Cody did not include more western myth and tradition in the plays.[15] Cody, too, sensed that he still lacked the right formula for his type of showmanship.[16] The stage limited his ability to express the majesty of the western frontier.

Unfortunately, the season ended on a tragic note. On April 20, 1876, just as the show was about to open in Springfield, Massachusetts, Cody received a telegram. It said that his only son, five-year-old Kit Carson Cody, was very ill with scarlet fever. Cody caught the nine o'clock train home to Rochester. Kit died that night in Cody's arms.

According to Cody's sister Helen, many of her brother's hopes died with his son.[17] Cody lost interest in acting and closed the show six weeks after Kit's death. He hoped to forget his grief by returning to the frontier. Cody could hardly have chosen a more dramatic time. For years, the Sioux were angrily protesting the broken Laramie Treaty. Signed in 1868, it gave the Black Hills of present-day South Dakota to the Sioux, who considered the area sacred. In 1874, rumors of gold in the hills began to spread. Swarms of gold-seekers rushed to the Black Hills. By 1876, thousands of warriors had gathered to defend the land that the treaty granted them.

A Famous Battle

By May, General Sheridan had assembled troops to battle the Sioux and their allies, the Cheyenne. He planned to have three columns attack at the

This is the only known photograph of Kit Carson Cody, taken when he was five. Soon after, he became ill with scarlet fever and died.

same time from three different directions. But his plan failed because General Custer would not wait to attack. On June 25, 1876, the Sioux slaughtered Custer and his troops near the Little Bighorn River in Montana at a battle that is often called "Custer's Last Stand."

In the meantime, Cody had joined the 5th Cavalry. Just as they prepared to move out, they received the spine-tingling news of Custer's defeat. One thousand Cheyenne warriors were on their way to join the Sioux. The 5th Cavalry went to head them off at Hat Creek near present-day Montrose, Nebraska. On July 17, 1876, Cody led a detachment of soldiers against a group of Cheyenne and fought his famous duel with the Cheyenne chief Yellow Hair (also called Yellow Hand). Cody and Yellow Hair approached each other on horseback. Cody's shot went through Yellow Hair's leg and killed his pinto pony. Cody's horse stumbled, but he jumped off and fired a second time. This shot killed Yellow Hair, and Cody left the battlefield with the brave's scalp.

After the military campaign ended, Cody returned to the stage. The Combination presented a play called *The Red Right Hand; or, Buffalo Bill's First Scalp for Custer*. It was based on Cody's battle with Yellow Hair. He advertised the play by displaying Yellow Hair's scalp and headdress. When

On July 17, 1876, Buffalo Bill led a small group of soldiers against Yellow Hair. He later used the battle as a theme in his performances. This scene shows him reenacting the scalping of Yellow Hair. He holds up the chief's war bonnet as a victory sign.

clergy members protested, Cody stopped the display. This increased interest in the show, because curious audiences then had to come to the theater to see the objects.[18] This play pointed to Buffalo Bill's future in outdoor western shows.[19] Horses and a trained donkey appeared. Cody and several other marksmen performed shooting exhibitions.

In the summer of 1877, Buffalo Bill's company successfully toured California and the West in the first presentation of a western show in the far

West.[20] When the tour finished, Cody visited a reservation and hired some Sioux for the next season, perhaps the first time a western show included real Native Americans. This tradition became an important step in the building of Buffalo Bill's future Wild West shows.[21]

At the end of the 1877 season, the first of many problems developed between Cody and his wife, Louisa. After Buffalo Bill paid four actresses who had performed in his Combination, he kissed them good-bye. Louisa was furious. Cody could not understand why his wife was angry. He thought she should be proud that his company members liked him so much.[22]

In 1878, Louisa and Orra traveled with the Combination while Arta attended a girls' boarding school in Rochester, New York. Louisa and Buffalo Bill may have gotten over their quarrel regarding him kissing the actresses. Or Louisa may have decided to travel with the company because she did not trust her husband.[23] However, after five months, Louisa became tired of the constant travel. She took Orra to North Platte, Nebraska, where Cody built a large new home called Welcome Wigwam. Although Louisa made North Platte her home for the next thirty-five years, Buffalo Bill spent little time there because of his travel schedule and a desire to avoid arguments with his wife.[24]

A Successful New Idea

As he became more famous, Cody realized that all his plays followed a similar formula. They were colorful spectacles with Native American dances and shooting exhibitions. Cody began to form an idea for a new kind of performance that would not be restricted to the stage. It would depict western history as he and others had experienced it.[25] In 1882, he met actor Nate Salsbury, who also had a new show idea. Salsbury hoped to bring an exhibition of horsemanship to Europe. He wanted a famous person to head up his show and felt Cody was the right man for the job. Yet neither had enough money to form a partnership.

In the summer of 1882, Cody went home to North Platte, where he created an Independence Day celebration called the "Old Glory Blow Out." Because it included riding, shooting, and bronc busting, this celebration marked the start of the Wild West show and was also one of the earliest rodeos.[26] Cody persuaded townspeople to offer prizes for these events. He publicized the contests with five thousand handbills, expecting about a hundred cowboys to appear. A whopping one thousand entered. The showstopper of the performance was the holdup of a stagecoach called the Deadwood Stage. The show's popularity convinced Buffalo Bill that he had found his formula for success.

6

BUFFALO BILL'S WILD WEST

Buffalo Bill Cody first discussed his idea for a Wild West show with General Sheridan in 1872. The general did not encourage him. "First thing you know some of those bucking broncos would buck into the audience and kill a couple of people," he said. "Or else the buffalo would stampede and there'd be all kinds of trouble."[1]

Sheridan's opinion proved wrong. Flush with his success after the "Old Glory Blow Out," Cody started hiring acts for his new outdoor show. In the meantime, he continued his theater tour for the 1882–1883 season. The tour took him to New York, where he again met with Nate Salsbury. Salsbury was still not ready to invest in a show. Soon after, Cody met with well-known marksman Dr. W. F. Carver, who agreed to form a partnership. Cody telegraphed Salsbury, inviting him to be their third partner. Salsbury declined, saying "Doc" Carver made false claims about his frontier adventures.

The new partnership started with trouble. The partners could not agree on a name for the show. Carver suggested "The Golden West." Cody named the show "The Wild West, Hon. W. F. Cody and Dr. W. F. Carver's Rocky Mountain and Prairie Exhibition." Carver later falsely claimed that the entire concept of the Wild West show was his idea.[2]

On May 19, 1883, the show opened to about eight thousand excited spectators in Omaha, Nebraska. Famous sports announcer "Pop" Whitaker served as ringmaster. The program set the standard for what became tradition in Cody's Wild West shows. It included the Pony Express and the Attack Upon the Deadwood Stage. Cody put on a shooting exhibition, as did Captain Adam H. Bogardus. Carver was listed on the program as "The Evil Spirit of the Plains."[3] He claimed that Native Americans had given him the title because he impressed them with his talents. Carver soon lived up to the name, showing an evil temper.[4] During a show at Coney Island, New York, Carver missed several shots. He was so furious that he smashed his rifle over his horse's ears and also hit his assistant.

When the show played in Chicago, Cody visited Salsbury, who was performing in a theater there. Cody complained that he could no longer tolerate working with Carver. Yet even though the two partners fought often, their show was a huge success. *The Hartford Courant* called it "the best open-air show ever seen."[5]

Before any changes could be made, Cody got more bad news. His eleven-year-old daughter Orra Maude was very ill. She died on October 24, 1883. His family was reduced to his two remaining daughters, sixteen-year-old Arta and baby Irma, who was born on February 9, 1883. Cody felt discouraged about the direction his life should take.[6] Rumors spread that he was drinking more, and his relationship with his wife worsened.[7]

Carver began to get jealous that Cody received more praise than he did. When Carver suggested they form a winter tour, Cody refused. They flipped a coin and divided up everything they jointly owned. Luckily, Cody got to keep the Deadwood Stage. It became one of the most popular parts of his Wild West show, and he used it in every single performance.

The Wild West

Cody formed a new partnership with Nate Salsbury, one that continued for nineteen years. They made an ideal team. Cody excelled as a showman, and Salsbury was a skillful business manager. Major John Burke continued as publicity chief.

The show played to large, enthusiastic crowds, but doing one-day stands became too expensive. The partners decided to try a full winter season in just one location. They chose New Orleans. With the show gear loaded on a river steamer, the move got underway. Then calamity struck. The show's steamboat collided with another boat. Within an hour, it sank to the bottom of the Mississippi River. Except for the Deadwood Stage and the bandwagon, all of the wagons, guns, ammunition, and show gear were lost. Cast members were able to rescue the horses, but the donkeys, buffalo, and elk drowned.

Salsbury was in Denver at the time, performing with his acting group. Cody telegraphed him: "Outfit at bottom of river, what do you advise?" Salsbury was about to go on stage to sing. He asked the orchestra to replay the overture so that he could decide on his answer. Salsbury wrote the following: "Go to New Orleans, reorganize, and open on your date."[8]

The situation presented an opportunity for Cody to prove his leadership and showmanship. In eight days, he obtained herds of buffalo and elk, wagons, and all the other necessary equipment. The show opened on time. After such a great organizational feat, Buffalo Bill deserved good luck. But bad weather struck instead. For forty-four straight days, it rained. Attendance was so poor that for one performance, only nine people came. Cody proved his showmanship by insisting that the performance go on. He said, "If nine people came out here in all this rain to see us, we'll show."[9]

Little Sure Shot

A bit of good luck shone through the New Orleans rain. The Sells Brothers Circus had been performing there at the same time. Some of its performers visited the Wild West. One of them was Annie Oakley, who had beaten the famous marksman Frank Butler in a shooting contest and later married him. After their marriage, they formed a shooting act called Butler and Oakley. During performances, Butler held Oakley's targets and loaded guns. He also managed her business affairs very well.

The Butlers approached Cody and Salsbury about joining the Wild West. At the time, the show already had several shooting acts. Later, when A. H. Bogardus left, Butler asked if they could put their act on trial for three days. Oakley later wrote, "I went right in and did my best before 17,000 people and was engaged in fifteen minutes."[10] After seeing

Another Annie Oakley

In her performances, Annie Oakley used a card target that was 2" x 5" in size. At one end, it had a picture of Oakley. At the other end was a heart-shaped bull's-eye. Once Oakley had hit the cards, they were thrown into the audience as souvenirs. Eventually, a free, prepunched admission ticket became known as an "Annie Oakley" because the punched hole looked like the bullet hole through Oakley's targets.

her perform, Salsbury put her name on the show's billing, a rare honor. He also ordered seven thousand dollars worth of extra advertising featuring Oakley.

On the show billing, Annie Oakley appeared as "The Peerless Wing and Rifle Shot," but she became more famous as "Little Sure Shot."[11] Sioux Chief Sitting Bull gave her the nickname. He had seen her perform in 1884 when he was on a tour of fifteen cities with other Sioux. He was so excited about the accuracy of her aim that he began to yell "Watanya Cicilla," meaning "Little Sure Shot." He thought she was filled with the Good Spirit, who gave her such true aim. At the show's end, the two exchanged photographs, and Sitting Bull adopted Oakley as his daughter.

Cody invited Sitting Bull to join the show. At first he refused. Then Major Burke spotted Oakley's photo in Sitting Bull's tepee. He told the chief he would see her every day if he performed with the Wild West. On June 6, 1885, Sitting Bull signed a contract for a four-month tour. He earned fifty dollars per week plus the right to sell his photographs and autographs. Like many performers and sports stars today, he also received a signing bonus. His was $125!

Buffalo Bill treated Sitting Bull with dignity throughout his entire time with the show. Cody presented him as Sitting Bull, the famous Sioux Chief, not as a leader of the same tribe that had killed Custer at the Little Bighorn.[12] Buffalo Bill said, "The whole secret of treating with Indians is to be honest with them and do as you agree."[13] He asked Sitting Bull to continue to tour, but the chief wanted to return to his people. When Sitting Bull left, Cody gave him the gray horse he had used in the show. It knelt down and lifted its hoof at the sound of gunfire. Cody also gave the chief a white sombrero, which Sitting Bull treasured until his death.[14]

A Winning Formula

The 1885 season proved that Buffalo Bill had a successful show idea. With a million spectators in all, the crowds broke attendance records, and the

*Sitting Bull appeared in the Wild West in 1885. The Sioux chief
trusted Cody and considered him a friend.*

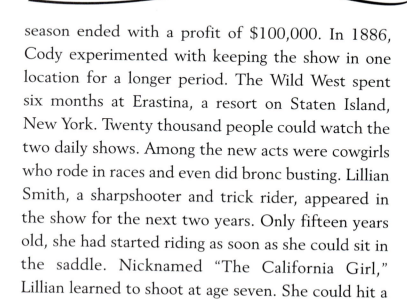

Sitting Bull

When the Wild West show toured the United States, crowds booed Sioux Chief Sitting Bull. They viewed him as an enemy because his people had defeated Custer. Yet they formed long lines to get his autograph, sold for one dollar each. They seemed to see him in the same way they saw Buffalo Bill. Like Cody, Sitting Bull was a legend in his own time, one who had lived in North America before it became "civilized."[15]

Sitting Bull enjoyed the attention he received, ignoring the boos. In the cities, he observed poverty that shocked him. As he told Annie Oakley, much of the money he made "went into the pockets of small, ragged boys."[16] Sitting Bull could not understand how whites could ignore the problems of their own poor. "The white man knows how to make everything, but he does not know how to distribute it," he said.[17]

season ended with a profit of $100,000. In 1886, Cody experimented with keeping the show in one location for a longer period. The Wild West spent six months at Erastina, a resort on Staten Island, New York. Twenty thousand people could watch the two daily shows. Among the new acts were cowgirls who rode in races and even did bronc busting. Lillian Smith, a sharpshooter and trick rider, appeared in the show for the next two years. Only fifteen years old, she had started riding as soon as she could sit in the saddle. Nicknamed "The California Girl," Lillian learned to shoot at age seven. She could hit a plate thirty times in fifteen seconds and shoot glass balls that hung from strings swinging from a pole.

The success of staying in one location encouraged Cody to lease New York's Madison Square Garden for an immense indoor show during the winter. The ceiling was raised twenty-five feet to make room for the gigantic stage sets. On opening night, nine thousand spectators filled the auditorium. As the lights dimmed, viewers heard the startling noise of horses' hooves indoors. Cody's voice filled the Garden: "Ladies and Gentlemen:

The Attack on a Settler's Cabin was always a hit with Wild West show spectators.

The Wild West presents the unique and unparalleled spectacle of Western life—The Drama of Civilization."[18] It was a colorful mix of cowboys, shooting exhibitions, a stagecoach, the Pony Express, Native Americans, a prairie fire, and a reenactment of Custer's Last Stand. A two-hundred-horsepower wind machine created a cyclone that blew down the buildings in Deadwood City and scattered one hundred bags of dried leaves across the stage.

After watching the show for two days in a row, Mark Twain, the American author, praised it for appearing to be so true to life, saying: "It brought vividly back the breezy, wild life of the great plains and the Rocky Mountains. . . . Down to its smallest details, the show is genuine cowboys, *vaqueros*, Indians, stage coach, costumes, and all. . . ."[19] Buffalo Bill's Wild West had conquered America. Now he looked for new worlds to conquer.

7

EUROPEAN ADVENTURES

In 1887, Queen Victoria of England planned to celebrate her Golden Jubilee, honoring the fiftieth year of her reign. At the same time, American organizers were planning the American Exhibition, featuring the Wild West show. Bringing the show to England changed Cody from an American hero to an international one.

The show company sailed from New York on the *State of Nebraska*, a ship Buffalo Bill chose especially because of its name. He considered Nebraska his home state, and using a ship with the same name would bring extra publicity to the show.[1]

On board were over 200 passengers, 180 horses, 18 buffalo, 10 mules, 10 elk, 5 Texas steers, 4 donkeys, and 2 deer. Everyone except Annie Oakley suffered seasickness when a strong storm hit the ship. Black Elk, a Sioux holy man who was on board, reported that the Native Americans sang death songs and dressed in special costumes, because they were certain they would die.[2] Cody, who was seasick himself, could not comfort them. Thankfully, the storm lasted only two days. Soon after, the ship finished its seventeen-day crossing.

Three trains took the performers to Earl's Court in West London. The speed of the setup impressed the thousands who lined the walls, watching. By nine o'clock that night, the cast members could go to bed in their own tents. Work on the twenty-thousand-seat arena had already begun. But the British workers kept staring at Buffalo Bill with his long hair and mustache. Cody figured he had better keep out of sight if he wanted the work done by the show's opening on May 9.[3]

On May 5, 1887, Edward, Prince of Wales, the future king, came to a special rehearsal performance of the Wild West. He brought his family and royalty from Britain, France, Germany, and Denmark. Cody worried about how well the performance would go, because his Native American actors and a hundred of the Texas ponies had not appeared in the show before. Wet weather had left the arena grounds muddy. Cody wanted a chance for the cast to practice before a live audience.

The show began, as Cody depicted it, when:

> the Indians, yelling like fiends, galloped out . . . and swept round the enclosure like a whirlwind. The effect was instantaneous and electric. The prince rose from his seat and leaned eagerly over the front of the box, and the whole party thrilled at the spectacle.[4]

From that moment on, the show proved a success.

Performing for the Queen

The Prince of Wales praised the Wild West so highly that his mother, Queen Victoria, asked Cody to bring the show to Windsor Castle. Buffalo Bill explained that the show's size made moving it impossible. Queen Victoria then agreed to go to Earl's Court. The announcement shocked the public. After the death of her dear husband Prince Albert in 1861, she had kept herself in seclusion. For twenty-six years, she had never left Windsor Castle for any theater performance.

She and her royal party arrived at five o'clock on the afternoon of May 11. The show began when a horseman entered the arena, carrying the American flag. The queen rose from her seat and bowed deeply to the flag. Her entire group joined her in the salute. Cody said the company cheered in approval, because "For the first time in history, since the Declaration of Independence, a sovereign of Great Britain had saluted the star-spangled banner, and that banner was carried by a member of Buffalo Bill's Wild West!"[5]

Queen Victoria had planned to stay for just one hour. However, she soon forgot herself in the excitement of the show and watched the entire seventy-five-minute performance. The sixty-seven-year-old monarch commanded another viewing in June before her Golden Jubilee. Possibly more royal spectators watched this show than any other outdoor entertainment event before or since.[6] At least five kings, three crown princes (future kings), and many princes and princesses attended.[7]

Five of the royal viewers rode in the Deadwood Stage. Inside were the kings of Denmark, Greece, Belgium, and Saxony; and the Prince of Wales. Buffalo Bill drove the coach. The Prince of Wales, an avid poker player, commented, "Colonel, you never held four kings like these before." Cody answered, "I've held four kings, but four kings and the Prince of Wales make a royal flush, such as no man ever held before."[8] The prince enjoyed retelling Cody's joke.

After the queen's visit, newspapers reported that "the people considered it *the thing* to go to the show, and thousands were turned away."[9] Admission cost one to four shillings (about twenty-five cents to one dollar). The square dance done on horseback impressed Londoners. The bucking broncos were especially exciting. In the open arena, cowboys saddled and mounted the untamed horses. It took a tough rider to stay in the saddle.

Between shows, Buffalo Bill received invitations to many dinners and parties. Day in and day out, he put on two performances and visited with members of

The Cowboy

Buffalo Bill's Wild West helped make cowboys an important part of western mythology. Cody showed them roping Texas steers and taming wild bucking broncos. Wild West cowboys were brave, strong, honest men.

The word cowboy, however, did not always have a positive meaning. In the eighteenth century, when New York tenants who rebelled against their landowners were called cowboys, the term was meant in a critical way. During the American Revolution, people called cowboys showed their loyalty to King George and the British government by stealing cows from the Patriots. Again the term was used in a negative way.

Buffalo Bill changed the image of the cowboy from a negative one to a positive one. Many people at the time viewed cowboys as men with dusty, low-paying jobs. Cody pictured them as leaders in his myth of the West. Because of the Wild West, cowboys today are not remembered as cow thieves or kidnappers. They are seen as romantic heroes.

the audience afterward in camp. Some people, then and since, criticized Cody for drinking too much. Certainly, he did drink alcohol at times while relaxing, but he promised his partner Nate Salsbury that he would never be drunk before or during a show.[10] He wrote that to be a success in his business, a performer "*must* be perfectly reliable and *sober*."[11] Furthermore, the British found that he did not get drunk while he was in England.[12] Historians feel that most of the stories about Buffalo Bill's supposed drinking at that time came from fellow Nebraskans who were jealous of his success.[13]

International Triumph

The six-month London season ended on October 13, 1887. Annie Oakley left the company at this time, perhaps because she had difficulty getting along with Lillian Smith, the other female sharpshooter.[14] The company then went on a tour of Great Britain. In Birmingham, two cowboys raced two cyclists. For eight hours a day, they rode around a track at Islington. The cowboys changed horses every hour, using thirty altogether. The six-day race stayed close, but the cowboys won by two laps and two miles.

Manchester was the last stop of the season. At Salford race course, Cody built what he called the largest theater in the world, furnished with steam heating and electric lighting.[15] Show members performed seven episodes in front of giant backdrops that cost forty thousand dollars. As part of the show, a prairie fire threatened a wagon train. Other exciting scenes presented a stampede of wild animals and the re-creation of Custer's Last Stand. A cyclone, created by a gigantic propeller, destroyed Deadwood City.

After a final performance on May 5, 1888, the cast set sail for home. The voyage went smoothly except for the death of Cody's twenty-year-old horse, Old Charlie. The troupe arrived in New York on May 20 to a gigantic welcome at Staten Island. They went immediately to Erastina, the island resort, where the show opened a few weeks later. The *New York Evening Telegram* called Cody the "Hero of Two Continents."[16]

After a year in the United States, Cody took his show back to Europe. Annie Oakley rejoined the company, which performed first in Paris in May 1889. The troupe continued on to Spain, where Oakley and many members of the company became ill. As Christmas neared, influenza, smallpox, and typhoid fever swept through the camp. Frank Richmond, the show's popular announcer, died on Christmas Eve.

It took another month for the cast to recover their health. The Wild West then moved on to Italy, where Pope Leo XIII blessed a group representing the show. An Italian prince challenged the cowboys to ride his wild stallions. A reporter for the *New York Herald* wrote that the audience expected two or three cowboys to die in the attempt to ride the wild horses.[17] But the Wild West cowboys showed their own ferocity. In front of twenty thousand spectators, they lassoed, saddled, and calmed the stallions in only five minutes.

Sellout crowds watched the show in Germany, where Wild West interest was stronger than anywhere else in Europe. Long before Buffalo Bill's Wild West came to their country, Germans were fascinated with western dime novels. Nearly every major German city had its own Wild West club. Club members studied western history and put on Wild West shows.

Threatening Rumors

While the Wild West was in Germany, newspapers reported that the show's management mistreated its Native American performers. White Horse, a former Native American actor in the Wild West, described to a *New York Herald* reporter the cruel treatment and starvation conditions he claimed to have suffered. Major Burke invited three top German officials to inspect the Native Americans and their living conditions. All three agreed that they were "the best looking, and apparently the best fed Indians we have ever seen."[18]

Buffalo Bill and Major Burke decided to bring home all the Native Americans to further disprove the rumors of mistreatment. Burke brought the Native Americans to the Bureau of Indian Affairs in Washington, D.C. The rest of the cast stayed behind in winter quarters in Alsace-Lorraine, France. In Washington, D.C., Rocky Bear and Red Dog spoke for their fellow Sioux, praising their treatment during their travels. The bureau dismissed all charges against Buffalo Bill and the Wild West.[19]

Buffalo Bill had intended to join Burke in Washington, but General Nelson Miles needed his advice about a possible Sioux war. Some of Sitting Bull's followers had taken up a new religion called the Ghost Dance. It taught that a savior would restore the land and the buffalo to the Native Americans. All whites would vanish, and Native Americans would be reunited with their ancestors.

Miles asked Cody to bring Sitting Bull to him to talk about the problem. Cody felt he could convince his friend to meet with the general. Unfortunately, Indian Agent James McLaughlin thought he could handle the situation better with tribal police, a group of Sioux chosen to keep order on the reservation. On December 18, 1890, Sitting Bull died when a fight broke out between his followers and the tribal police. When Sitting Bull's gray horse from the Wild West show heard the shots, it knelt and lifted its hoof several times. People watching thought that Sitting Bull had entered its body, causing the horse to do a ghost dance.[20] Later the horse was returned to Cody and used in the show again. Buffalo Bill was one of the few white men Sitting Bull ever considered his friend, but McLaughlin's actions prevented Cody from helping the chief.[21]

Expanding the Show

While Cody was in America, Salsbury remained in Europe and hired new horse-riding acts. The performers included soldiers from the United States, Britain, France, Germany, and Russia, as well as Syrian and Arab horsemen. The partners changed the show title to "Buffalo Bill's Wild West and Congress of Rough Riders of the World." The bigger and better show toured Holland and Belgium and closed in London on October 12, 1892, ending nearly three and a half years in Europe.

At the end of the European tour, planning began immediately for the World's Columbian Exposition. The Exposition was a world's fair being held in Chicago to honor the four-hundredth anniversary of Christopher Columbus's arrival in North America. Buffalo Bill's Wild West and Congress of Rough Riders of the World was not

Partners Buffalo Bill and Nate Salsbury added exciting acts of horsemanship to their show and renamed it "Buffalo Bill's Wild West and Congress of Rough Riders of the World." Rosa Bonheur, pictured in the center of this poster, helped publicize the show with her many oil paintings of Buffalo Bill.

invited to take part. The fair organizers felt the show was not the dignified kind of cultural presentation they wished to feature.[22] Nate Salsbury, however, had planned ahead and leased a lot near the main entrance to the fair, and the Wild West set up there.

Buffalo Bill's show opened on April 3, 1893, in pouring rain. However, no performances had to be canceled during the 186-day season, making it one of the most successful outdoor shows in history.[23] The grandstand seated eighteen thousand, but still the ticket takers often had to turn away viewers.

Hints of Trouble

The 1893 and 1894 shows appeared similar, but, thanks to the Chicago exhibition, the 1893 season brought in nearly $1 million more. By 1894, many

A New Show Idea

In 1895, Buffalo Bill invested in Nate Salsbury's new show, "an exposition of negro life and character, entitled 'Black America.'"[24] It was based on minstrel shows, programs with songs, dances, and jokes from African-American culture. Prior to this time, minstrel performers had been whites who blackened their faces with stage makeup. Cody and Salsbury felt the timing was right for African-American actors to perform these numbers. They sent three hundred African Americans on tour in fifteen railroad cars.

The show failed after only three weeks. "Black America" tried to show the drama of African-American life. But it did not fit a Wild West format. Also, its presentation took place only thirty years after the end of the Civil War. Viewers, especially those living in the South, may not yet have been ready to accept African-American performers. Thus, "Black America" seemed to be an idea that was ahead of its time.[25]

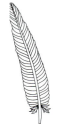

individuals and businesses were experiencing financial problems. They could not afford to come to the show. Buffalo Bill's expenses totalled four thousand dollars per day, and he had difficulty meeting them. By 1894, he was nearly bankrupt.

That same year, Nate Salsbury became seriously ill. He brought in James A. Bailey from the Barnum and Bailey Circus to manage the show. With Bailey in charge, the show returned to one-day stands. In 1895, the troupe traveled nine thousand miles, performing 131 one-day stands in 190 days.[26]

By 1896, Cody was tired of the constant travel. At age fifty, he was beginning to have trouble with his health, but he had to keep working to cover his many investments. He now owned two ranches: Scout's Rest in North Platte, Nebraska, near Louisa's Welcome Wigwam home, and the TE Ranch in the Bighorn Basin of Wyoming. His grand scheme for the basin included a huge irrigation canal, a road into Yellowstone Park, and a lodge by the park entrance.

In 1898, the Spanish-American War broke out in Cuba. Although he was fifty-two years old, Cody offered his services to General Nelson A. Miles. By the time Miles reached Cuba, though, the war was nearly over. He told Cody to stay home, because his partners and employees depended on him for their income. Still, Cody felt his image was tarnished by failing to serve.[27]

Troubles continued to mount for Cody and his show. In less than two years, the Wild West train suffered three damaging wrecks. The third one, on October 28, 1901, killed more than one hundred horses, including one of Cody's favorite mounts, Old Pap. The crash also severely injured Annie Oakley. She remained in the hospital for several months and never again appeared with Buffalo Bill's Wild West.

The most serious blow of all took place on Christmas Eve, 1902. Just as he was about to begin that year's London season, Cody received word of Nate Salsbury's death. This left Cody on his own. What would happen to Buffalo Bill now that he had lost his trusted business partner?

THE SCOUT'S LAST STAND

In 1902, Buffalo Bill turned fifty-six years old. His show's one-day stands made him more and more tired. He wanted to retire from the Wild West, but he was too much in debt to do so.[1] A terrible business decision Cody made in 1902 added to his debts. Colonel D. B. Dyer, a former government agent for Native American affairs, convinced Cody to invest with him in the Campo Bonito Mine in Oracle, Arizona. The mine supposedly contained gold, lead, and tungsten. (Tungsten was used in electrical lighting and for hardening steel.) From 1902 to 1912, Cody poured half a million dollars into the mine, hoping to strike it rich, but he never made a profit.

His Wild West went on its second European tour from 1902 to 1906. It began on December 26, 1902, in Earl's Court, the site of its first London season in 1887. The early crowds were large and enthusiastic, but then attendance declined. Business picked up in 1903 after King Edward VII and Queen Alexandra of England visited. Edward had become king when his mother, Queen Victoria, died in 1901. A new act, George Davis, the "Cowboy Cyclist," also heightened interest in the show. Davis jumped his bicycle over a "chasm of 56 feet, covering a distance, in the plunge of 171 feet."[2]

Divorce Threatened

In 1904, problems resurfaced in Cody's marriage. Relations between Buffalo Bill and Louisa hit a low point when their daughter Arta died on January 30, 1904. She was to be buried in Rochester, New York, beside Kit and Orra, the other two Cody children who had died. Cody urged his wife to forget their past differences, but in the train on the way to the funeral, Louisa "replied by accusing him of breaking Arta's heart and causing her death."[3] Although these charges were untrue, Louisa continued to fight with her husband. When the train stopped in

Chicago, she made a scene at the Auditorium Hotel, criticizing Buffalo Bill and his sisters.

In February and March 1905, the Cody divorce hearing took place. It seemed to be a contest to determine which of the Codys could bring the most ridiculous charges against the other. Buffalo Bill claimed that Louisa nagged him constantly. He also charged that she had tried to poison him the day after Christmas, 1900. Louisa supposedly used Dragon's Blood, a love potion from a gypsy. Witnesses described Louisa's jealousy of the Wild West actresses.

Cody's most serious charge against Louisa regarded her handling of money. All during his performing career, he sent funds to Louisa so that she could purchase property. In 1882, Cody learned that Louisa had purchased all of the property in her name alone. He wrote to his sister Julia in 1883 that Louisa "has tried to ruin me financially this summer."[4] Louisa distrusted Cody's ability to manage finances, with good reason.[5] Cody had trouble saving money. He had also made a series of bad investments in products such as a cough medicine and a coffee substitute called Panamalt. Cody's attempt to fund a colony in Mexico had failed, and his Campo Bonito Mine in Arizona continually drained his finances.

In presenting her side of the case, Louisa accused

Cody of drinking too much. From the statements of witnesses at the trial, it appeared that Louisa felt abandoned by the family on the trip to bury Arta.[6] She also believed that Cody wanted to make up with her only until the funeral was over.

There was probably some truth in the claims of both Buffalo Bill and Louisa. Cody did have difficulty saving money; therefore, it was natural for his wife to guard their financial resources. It was also understandable that Cody would be angry when he discovered that she had purchased property in her name only. Cody was very generous to his sisters, which caused resentment on Louisa's part. The divorce hearing strained their relationships with both friends and family members. All in all, the actions and words of both Louisa and Buffalo Bill diminished their reputations. The judge finally decided in favor of Louisa and ordered Cody to pay Louisa's court costs, a total of $318.

Disputes between Louisa and Buffalo Bill continued until 1910 when his show played in North Platte, Nebraska. Their grandson convinced the couple to meet privately in a room at Welcome Wigwam. When they came out of the room, the couple had agreed to try again to make their marriage work.

In their later years, Buffalo Bill and Louisa Cody got along better in their marriage and enjoyed spending time with their grandchildren.

Ups and Downs

From April 2 to June 4, 1905, Buffalo Bill took the Wild West to Paris and enjoyed huge financial success there. Artillery and cavalry from several countries performed maneuvers, or drills. Appearing were veterans of the United States Cavalry as well as Arab, Japanese, French, and English soldiers.

Unfortunately, further troubles beset Cody in 1905. A gland disease first appeared among the show's horses on July 10. By season's end, two hundred out of the three hundred Wild West mounts had died.

The following year, James Bailey died suddenly. Bailey had handled the show's scheduling and transportation in return for a share of the profits. In Bailey's papers, his relatives found an I.O.U. note from Cody for twelve thousand dollars. Cody said he had paid the debt, and he was always truthful in such matters.[7] He had no proof, however, and Bailey's heirs expected repayment. Bailey's death put additional pressure on Buffalo Bill's Wild West and Congress of Rough Riders of the World to produce a profit. Cody could not retire until he paid off his debt to the Bailey family.

A week after Bailey's death, the show opened in Marseille, France, where it was very successful. The company then moved on to Italy, Austria, Hungary, and Germany. After a short stop in Belgium, the season ended in France on October 30, 1906.

The next year, Buffalo Bill put together his first American tour in five years. He planned the show himself. He used many of his tried-and-true acts, such as the robbery of the Deadwood Stage, and introduced the reenactment of the Battle of Summit Springs. Another new act was "The Great Train Hold-up and Bandit Hunters of the Union Pacific." It included a locomotive, built over an early version of the automobile, that could be driven onstage.

Help from Pawnee Bill

In 1908, Cody joined forces with Major Gordon Lillie, known as Pawnee Bill. His show, Pawnee Bill's Historic Far West and Great Far East, needed the fame of Buffalo Bill's name. Cody needed Lillie's money. They combined to create "Buffalo Bill's Wild West combined with Pawnee Bill's Great Far East." Cast members nicknamed it the Two Bills Show. It featured a new act, "Football on Horseback."[8] Five Native Americans and five cowboys charged toward a six-foot round ball. Each group tried to put it across the goal line before the opposition could push it back.

In 1909, Bailey's relatives sold their share of Buffalo Bill's Wild West to Gordon Lillie, canceling the twelve-thousand-dollar debt Cody owed Bailey.

Lillie was now the sole owner of the Two Bills Show. Even so, he treated Buffalo Bill with respect, because he knew that Buffalo Bill's reputation was what drew crowds to the show.[9] Lillie made Cody his partner and paid Cody's share of the partnership out of the show's earnings.

Buffalo Bill hoped to have enough money saved so that he could retire in 1910. He gave a touching farewell speech on May 14, 1910, at Madison Square Garden. Although Cody truly meant every word of the speech, he could not meet his retirement goal.[10] The show earned a profit of four hundred thousand dollars that year, but Cody spent most of his share on his mine in Arizona. He had to extend his "Farewell Exhibitions" through 1912 and also sold his Scout's Rest Ranch to Lillie to pay more of his debts. It was not enough. At the end of the 1912 season, Cody still owed Lillie twenty thousand dollars to cover his half of the show's winter housing costs. Buffalo Bill did not have the funds.

Deeper in Debt

He then made a fateful decision. On a visit to his sister in Denver in November 1912, Cody met Harry H. Tammen, co-owner of the *Denver Post* and owner of the small Sells-Floto Circus. Tammen wanted to become powerful enough to compete with the Ringling Brothers, who owned the largest circus at that time. Tammen was glad to lend money to Buffalo Bill, because Tammen intended to take over the Two Bills Show. He wanted the prestige of Buffalo Bill's name and reputation. He planned to build a circus empire by combining Buffalo Bill's Wild West with the Sells-Floto Circus. Tammen announced in the *Denver Post* that Buffalo Bill would join with the Sells-Floto Circus in 1914. Pawnee Bill (Gordon Lillie) would not be a part of the new show. In actuality, no such agreement had been signed. Tammen just wanted Lillie to think that Buffalo Bill had cheated him. The plan worked. Lillie was furious with Buffalo Bill. The Two Bills Show continued to tour, but Lillie refused to cover any more of Cody's debts. This action left Buffalo Bill deeper in Tammen's control.

Cody planned to pay off his loan to Tammen using the profits from the Two Bills' 1913 season. But 1913 was a disastrous year. Heavy rains and small crowds put Cody deeper in debt. Tammen did not care. What he really wanted was Buffalo Bill's name and fame. When the show came to Denver, Tammen got the sheriff to shut it down. The animals and show gear were auctioned off to pay Cody's debts. Cody called Tammen "the man who had my show sold at sheriff's sale, which broke my heart."[11]

The proud showman, however, was not defeated. He came up with a plan of producing a series of eight historical films about the West. He hired Native Americans and cowboys to reenact events such as the killing of Yellow Hair and the Battle of Wounded Knee. Cody toured briefly with the films. Though the idea was creative, it did not make much money.

In 1914, mounting debts forced Cody to appear with Tammen's circus. Buffalo Bill did not shoot or perform in any acts. He just rode into the ring and introduced the show. At age sixty-eight, he often had to be helped onto his horse. Once he was in the spotlight, though, Buffalo Bill sat tall in the saddle, as he had always done. The old showman, his hair now white, still presented the spectators with a living legend. Cody toured with the circus for two years. Then in 1916, he appeared with the Miller and Arlington Wild West Show. Cody's final performance was on November 4, 1916.

Scout's Rest

He then went to visit his sister in Denver, Colorado. From there, he traveled to his Wyoming ranch. In December, Buffalo Bill returned to Denver, where he caught a bad cold and soon developed severe complications. When his wife Louisa and daughter Irma arrived in Denver, Cody's condition had improved. He suffered setbacks, however, and died on January 10, 1917, at the age of seventy.

For two days, Cody's body lay in state, displayed in his bronze casket. The casket was positioned in the rotunda, the large central area of the capitol dome in Denver. More than twenty-five thousand people filed by to honor him. A group of seventy cowboys marched in his funeral procession. Two of them led Cody's white horse, McKinley, with its saddle empty, reins loose, and pistols hanging from the saddle horn. At Cody's funeral service, tribute was paid to the man whose friends included "presidents, kings, czars, and royalty to the millions of common people" and who had "the courage of a lion" and "the heart of a child."[12]

Controversy developed immediately about his burial location. Louisa said that Cody had wanted to be buried on Lookout Mountain near Denver, Colorado. Supposedly Cody's will stated that he wanted to be buried on a mountain site near Cody, Wyoming. For almost five months, arguments continued. In the meantime, Cody's body was kept at Denver's Olinger Mortuary in a crypt, or underground burial chamber.

Louisa insisted that her husband be buried on Lookout Mountain. Harry Tammen, co-owner of the *Denver Post* and the man who had sold Buffalo Bill's show, paid for the funeral and burial expenses. Many historians feel Tammen may have pressured Louisa into choosing Denver as the burial site, since Cody died in debt to the publisher and circus owner.[13]

The town of Cody, Wyoming, dedicated its own monument to Buffalo Bill. "The Scout" was carved by Gertrude Vanderbilt Whitney. Today the statue and a museum are among the town's tributes to its namesake.

Officials of Cody, Wyoming, were disappointed that Buffalo Bill would not be buried in the city he had founded. They built their own monument to him. Titled "The Scout," it is a twelve-foot bronze statue of Cody astride his horse.

After the winter snows had melted, Buffalo Bill was buried on June 3, 1917, on Lookout Mountain in Colorado. A tomb had been carved out of the solid granite mountain top. Three thousand cars drove seven and a half miles up the winding road to the crest of the mountain. The *Denver Post* reported that twenty-five thousand people came to the burial. It took two hours for them to file past Cody's grave.[14] His funeral was nearly as large a spectacle as many of his Wild West shows, something the old scout probably would have enjoyed.

FACT OR FICTION

Like all legendary figures, Buffalo Bill was a complex mix of fact and fiction. Who was the real man behind the myth? A skilled scout, he was modest about his abilities. He possessed great physical endurance and a vast knowledge of Native American ways. With his sense of humor, Buffalo Bill never took himself too seriously. He loved his children and showed kindness to orphans and the children of his cast members. His flair for showmanship made him popular with audiences all over the world. Yet he had difficulty getting along with his wife. He was so generous that he could not stay out of debt. He probably drank too much, yet his drinking never interfered with his keeping a job. All in all, Buffalo Bill was a human being with many virtues and his share of faults.

How did this ordinary human being become a legend? Writers often exaggerated to make his life more interesting and exciting, as if Buffalo Bill's true deeds were not exciting enough. Plays and dime novels about him were full of fantastic detail. Some writers admired Buffalo Bill highly and wanted to publicize his show and his life. Family members wrote to present their points of view. Cody wrote four exciting books about himself, some parts of which were more accurate than others.[1] Over the years, the details of once-true stories became muddled and exaggerated. So, when audiences came to his show, they already had a romantic picture of Buffalo Bill and the West that was not entirely based on facts.

Buffalo Bill's Wild West advertised itself as genuine, because Cody felt he had a mission to educate the public about western history.[2] In an effort to make his acts more thrilling, though, he sometimes took liberties with history. For example, Buffalo Bill was not present at Custer's Last Stand, but in the reenactment, he arrived at the end of the battle. A spotlight shone on him. The words "Too late!" flashed on a screen. Buffalo Bill romanticized the actual event of Custer's death to make it more dramatically appealing.

With such actions, Buffalo Bill developed his own identity that was part real, part fictitious.[3] Acts in his Wild West show and actual history constantly imitated each other. The Wild West performances seemed more real because Cody had lived these events.[4] His show included Native Americans who had also lived the events. For example, some of the Sioux who fought General Custer at the Little Bighorn later appeared in the Wild West re-creation of the battle. In the Wild West programs, Cody published letters from famous military officers. They testified to his scouting skills and his participation in the battles the Wild West reenacted. Buffalo Bill left the show to serve as an Army scout, and when he returned, he added parts of his experiences to the show. In his shows, it was never quite clear where the reenactment of an event stopped and true life started.[5] For his audiences, fact and fiction blended, as Buffalo Bill's Wild West became the myth of the legendary western frontier.

Important Parts of the Western Myth

Native Americans played a vital role in Buffalo Bill's Wild West and the myth of the West. Illustrations of many tribes, including the Arapaho, Cheyenne, and Sioux, appeared in show advertising and programs.

Cody tried to give the tribes dignity, introducing each one and announcing its chief or leader.[6] However, acts in the Wild West featured Native American aggression against white defenders. The warriors were killers and the whites were victims.[7] This viewpoint had been a common one since the first settlement of North America.

Still, Buffalo Bill's Wild West left the impression that although they had once been enemies, whites and Native Americans had to learn to get along in peace.[8] Cody wrote that he sympathized with the Native Americans and their struggle to keep their lands.[9] He urged the United States government to treat them more fairly. At the same time, though, he thought that "the march of civilization was inevitable, and that sooner or later the men who lived in roving tribes, making no real use of the resources of the country, would be compelled to give way before the men who tilled the soil."[10] Such a view was common at the time.

The settlement of the frontier doomed Native American culture. By 1890, tribes already experienced difficulty adjusting to their changed lives on the reservation. Appearing with Buffalo Bill offered them a chance to earn money. Some historians today feel that Native Americans may have been harmed by such performances. Buffalo Bill trapped them in a stereotype of warriors in war paint. As long as they were willing to play the parts of Native Americans as they once were, that was all they could do. Once they had seen life off the reservation, their own lives there looked even more dismal.[11]

Today movies and television portray Native Americans in feathered headdresses and on horseback, because that is the way they appeared in the Wild West.[12] Buffalo Bill used Sioux, who did wear feathered headdresses and ride ponies. Many other tribes, such as the Apache, did not wear feathers and rarely rode horses, yet all were portrayed in the same way.

Cowboys and Cowgirls

Buffalo Bill's Wild West helped make the cowboy into a myth. Real-life cowboys toiled long and hard on cattle drives. Show cowboys presented a more romantic version. They were knights on horseback, who always came to the rescue in time. Riding, roping, and shooting exhibitions showed audiences many of their skills. Spectators never saw the less glamorous side of their job.

The Wild West presented a variety of images of pioneer women. Women in the West rode and shot, and they operated ranches in several western states. Buffalo Bill tried to show western women the way he thought audiences wanted to see them.[13] The talents of Annie Oakley, Lillian Smith, and other

The Wild West and Rodeo

The Wild West influenced the development of the rodeo. The word rodeo comes from the Spanish word *rodear*, meaning "to surround." Rodeo includes five basic contests: saddle bronc riding, bareback bronc riding, calf roping, bull riding, and steer wrestling. Most rodeos also include several other events such as team roping, barrel racing, and steer roping.

Rodeo began with informal races and roundups whenever cowboys challenged each other. The first formal rodeo contest took place at a Fourth of July celebration in Cheyenne, Wyoming, in 1872. Buffalo Bill was right in step with the development of rodeo when he held his "Old Glory Blow Out" in 1882, where he scheduled a variety of events and offered prizes. The Cowboy Fun and lassoing demonstrations in the Wild West show were also part of the beginnings of rodeo. The 1916 Wild West performance in Chicago was billed as a rodeo. Today, about two thousand rodeos are held each year, mostly in the United States and Canada.

sharpshooters set them apart from eastern women. Yet they wore tailored costumes that still looked "ladylike." Georgia Duffy and Della Farrell, who did trick riding and bronc busting, appeared in split skirts. Native American women set up their village and reenacted the torture of captive white women. Thus, the Wild West showed both independent women and ones who needed protection. Television and movies later showed similar roles.[14]

A Living Legacy

Buffalo Bill once said, "I do not wish to be only known as a scout and showman, but as a pioneer and developer of civilization."[15] Buffalo Bill had great plans for the Bighorn Basin in Wyoming. Although most of them were not completed during his lifetime, today they are a legacy to his name. The Shoshone Dam was completed in 1910. It was renamed the Buffalo Bill Dam in 1946 and now supplies water to irrigation systems throughout the Bighorn Basin. The area has become the fine ranching country that Buffalo Bill dreamed it would be.

The legend of Buffalo Bill lives on in Cody, Wyoming, the town he founded in 1896. The Buffalo Bill Cody Stampede comes in July, followed by the Buffalo Bill Festival in August. Downtown is the Irma Hotel, which opened in 1902 and was named for Cody's daughter. Pahaska Tepee, Cody's first hunting lodge, still stands at the east entrance to Yellowstone National Park. The Buffalo Bill Historical Center contains four museums. Its Buffalo Bill Museum houses the largest collection of Buffalo Bill material in the world.

North Platte, Nebraska, holds its Old West Festival in June. Each year, the Buffalo Bill Award is given to an individual who contributes to family entertainment. Also in North Platte is Buffalo Bill's Ranch State Park. It includes the restored house, barn, and other buildings of the original Scout's Rest Ranch. The state park is maintained as a museum with furniture and mementos from Buffalo Bill's Wild West and his personal life.

The Buffalo Bill Memorial Museum and Grave are located atop Lookout Mountain in Golden, Colorado. The museum displays a large collection of Buffalo Bill materials. Special events include Buffalo Bill's birthday in February and Golden's annual Buffalo Bill Days Celebration in July.

Since Cody's death, many books, movies, and television shows have been made about him. Dime novels about Buffalo Bill and other heroes helped create a new type of book, the "western." Although fictional like the dime novel, westerns are not as sensational. Still, such books usually contain a hero and lots of action. Zane Grey and Louis L'Amour are among the writers famous for westerns.

The term "western" also applies to certain television shows and movies. A wealth of westerns have carried on the Buffalo Bill myth. Between 1923 and 1976 alone, thirty-five movies were made about Buffalo Bill. Most of them dwell on the exciting, sensational parts of Cody's life. Few have looked at the real man behind the legend.[16]

Buffalo Bill enjoyed meeting with children after the show. He never tired of posing for pictures and signing autographs.

Buffalo Bill's Role Today

As we enter the twenty-first century, how do we evaluate Buffalo Bill's contribution to history? Historians are continually reconsidering America's past history, looking at the treatment of African Americans, Hispanic Americans, and Native Americans in particular. They question how the settlement of the frontier misused resources, such as the buffalo, and destroyed the prairies. What was Buffalo Bill's role in this process? Certainly he killed buffalo, but he did not participate in their slaughter for hides. He loved the wide open spaces of the West, yet he also felt that whites were destined to settle there. Most likely, the excitement of his show encouraged many more people to move to the frontier. He worked with African-American soldiers and hired Hispanic and Native Americans for his show. Though he treated everyone in the Wild West with dignity, the show often tended to portray Native Americans as bloodthirsty. Buffalo Bill lived in an era of great change. He did what he thought was right. As a friend of his said, Buffalo Bill was a man of his times, and we should not judge him.[17]

Buffalo Bill sensed his historical importance. He had really lived the life of the Old West. He had been a trapper, Pony Express rider, stagecoach driver, and scout. His real-life adventures were transformed into his Wild West show. He called it an exhibition. To him it was educational, not a show or a circus.[18] Buffalo Bill and his Wild West represented one view of American history. They symbolized the West of wide open spaces, blue skies, herds of buffalo, and skilled cowboys and scouts. As the man behind the myth, Buffalo Bill had his faults. Not everyone will agree with his views. Still, we have him to thank for building a rich tradition of a romantic Wild West. In William F. Cody's own words, he wanted "to bring the people of the East and of the New West to the Old West, and possibly here and there to supply new material for history."[19]

CHRONOLOGY

1846—Born in LeClaire, Iowa, on February 26.

1853—Moved with his family to Salt Creek Valley in Kansas.

1860—Joined the Pony Express.

1864—Enlisted in the 7th Kansas Volunteer Cavalry to fight for the North in the Civil War.

1866—Married Louisa Frederici on March 6.

1867—Hired to supply buffalo meat for railroad workers.

1868—Hired as chief of scouts for the 5th Cavalry.

1869—Fought in the Battle of Summit Springs on July 11; First dime novel about Cody, Ned Buntline's *Buffalo Bill, the King of Border Men*, published.

1872—Guided Grand Duke Alexis of Russia on a hunting trip; Earned the Congressional Medal of Honor; Starred in *The Scouts of the Prairie*.

1875—First dime novel written by Cody, *The Pearl of the Prairies; or, The Scout and the Renegade*, published.

1876—Killed the Cheyenne chief Yellow Hair.

1882—Held the "Old Glory Blow Out" on July 4.

1883—Opened the Wild West on May 17.

1887—Appeared before Queen Victoria in London on May 11.

1889—First European tour of the Wild West (through 1892).

1893—Wild West played at the Columbian Exposition in Chicago for six months.

1902—Second European tour of the Wild West (through 1906).

1913—Wild West closed for nonpayment of debts on July 21.

1917—William F. "Buffalo Bill" Cody died in Denver, Colorado, on January 10.

CHAPTER NOTES

Chapter 1

1. B. A. Botkin, ed., *A Treasury of American Folklore* (New York: Crown Publishers, Inc., 1944), p. 151.

2. Shirl Kasper, *Annie Oakley* (Norman, Okla.: University of Oklahoma Press, 1992), p. 37.

3. Ibid.

4. William Frederick Cody, *An Autobiography of Buffalo Bill (Colonel W. F. Cody)* (New York: Holt, Rinehart and Winston, 1920), pp. 315–316.

5. Botkin, p. 151.

6. Robert Paul Walker, *Great Figures of the Wild West* (New York: Facts on File, Inc., 1992), p. 36.

7. Joseph G. Rosa and Robin May, *Buffalo Bill and His Wild West* (Lawrence, Kans.: University Press of Kansas, 1989), p. 87.

8. Don Russell, *The Lives and Legends of Buffalo Bill* (Norman, Okla.: University of Oklahoma Press, 1960) pp. 231–232.

9. Richard Slotkin, *Gunfighter Nation: The Myth of the Frontier in Twentieth-Century America* (New York: Atheneum, 1992), p. 72.

10. Walter Havighurst, *Annie Oakley of the Wild West* (Lincoln, Nebr.: University of Nebraska Press, 1992), p. 36; Glenda Riley, *The Life and Legacy of Annie Oakley* (Norman, Okla.: University of Oklahoma Press, 1994), pp. 145, 156.

11. Don Russell, *The Wild West* (Fort Worth, Tex.: Amon Carter Museum of Western Art, 1970), p. 25.

12. Kasper, p. 48.

13. Russell, *The Lives*, p. 319.

14. Paul O'Neil, *The End and the Myth* (Alexandria, Va.: Time-Life Books, Inc., 1979), p. 62.

15. Havighurst, p. 38.

16. Russell, *The Lives*, p. 438.

17. Nellie Snyder Yost, *Buffalo Bill: His Family, Fame, Failures, and Fortunes* (Chicago: The Swallow Press, Inc., 1979), p. 174.

18. Ibid.

Chapter 2

1. William Frederick Cody, *An Autobiography of Buffalo Bill (Colonel W. F. Cody)* (New York: Holt, Rinehart and Company, 1920), p. 5.

2. Ibid., pp. 5–6.

3. Don Russell, *The Lives and Legends of Buffalo Bill* (Norman, Okla.: University of Oklahoma Press, 1960), p. 25.

4. Joseph G. Rosa and Robin May, *Buffalo Bill and His Wild West* (Lawrence, Kans.: University Press of Kansas, 1989), p. 5.

5. William Frederick Cody, *The Life of Hon. William F. Cody Known As Buffalo Bill* (Lincoln, Nebr.: University of Nebraska Press, 1978), p. 55.

6. Ibid., p. 57.

7. Russell, p. 36.

8. Cody, *The Life*, p. 61.

9. Walter Havighurst, *Annie Oakley of the Wild West* (Lincoln, Nebr.: University of Nebraska Press, 1992), p. 63.

10. Ibid.

11. Cody, *The Life*, p. 72.

12. Don Cusic, *Cowboys and the Wild West* (New York: Facts on File, Inc., 1994), pp. 201–202.

13. Cody, *Autobiography*, p. 29.

14. Russell, pp. 47–48.

15. Cody, *The Life*, pp. 104–105; Russell, p. 50.

16. Cody, *Autobiography*, p. 45.

17. Cody, *The Life*, pp. 105–106.

Chapter 3

1. Don Russell, *The Lives and Legends of Buffalo Bill* (Norman, Okla.: University of Oklahoma Press, 1960), p. 55.

2. William Frederick Cody, *The Life of Hon. William F. Cody Known As Buffalo Bill* (Lincoln, Nebr.: University of Nebraska Press, 1978), pp. 125–126.

3. Ibid., p. 127.

4. Ibid.

5. Don Cusic, *Cowboys and the Wild West* (New York: Facts on File, Inc., 1994), p. 152.

6. Cody, p. 135.

7. Joseph G. Rosa and Robin May, *Buffalo Bill and His Wild West* (Lawrence, Kans.: University Press of Kansas, 1989), p. 8.

8. Ibid.

9. Cody, pp. 136–137.

10. Nellie Snyder Yost, *Buffalo Bill: His Family, Friends, Fame, Failures, and Fortunes* (Chicago: The Swallow Press, Inc., 1979), p. 11.

11. Ibid.

12. Paul O'Neil, *The End and the Myth* (Alexandria, Va.: Time-Life Books, Inc., 1977), p. 56.

13. Ibid.

14. Russell, p. 75.

15. Ibid., p. 76.

16. Yost, p. 12.

17. Ibid.

18. Helen Cody Wetmore, *Buffalo Bill: Last of the Great Scouts* (Chicago: The Duluth Press Publishing Company, 1899), p. 136.

Chapter 4

1. William Frederick Cody, *The Life of Hon. William F. Cody Known As Buffalo Bill* (Lincoln, Nebr.: University of Nebraska Press, 1978), p. 147.

2. Don Russell, *The Lives and Legends of Buffalo Bill* (Norman, Okla.: University of Oklahoma Press, Inc., 1979), p. 84.

3. Ibid., pp. 85–87.

4. Wayne Gard, *The Great Buffalo Hunt* (New York: Alfred A. Knopf, 1959), pp. 80–81.

5. Cody, pp. 154–155.

6. Robert Paul Walker, *Great Figures of the Wild West* (New York: Facts on File, Inc., 1992), p. 33.

7. Harold McCracken, *Winning of the West* (Garden City, N.Y.: Doubleday & Company, Inc., 1955), p. 60.

8. Russell, p. 87.

9. Nellie Snyder Yost, *Buffalo Bill: His Family, Friends, Fame, Failures, and Fortunes* (Chicago: The Swallow Press, Inc., 1979), p. 15.

10. Joseph G. Rosa and Robin May, *Buffalo Bill and His Wild West* (Lawrence, Kans.: University Press of Kansas, 1989), p. 18.

11. Ibid.

12. Russell, p. 151.

13. Don Cusic, *Cowboys and the Wild West* (New York: Facts on File, Inc., 1994), p. 49.

14. Don Russell, *The Wild West* (Fort Worth, Tex.: Amon Carter Museum of Western Art, 1970), p. 16.

15. Rosa and May, p. 27.

16. Keith Wheeler, *The Scouts* (Alexandria, Va.: Time-Life Books, Inc., 1978), pp. 7, 15.

17. Rosa and May, p. 33.

18. Ibid., p. 34.

19. Paul Fees, "In Defense of Buffalo Bill: A Look at Cody in and of His Time," *The Myth of the West*, ed. Chris Bruce, (Seattle, Wash.: University of Washington, 1990), p. 143.

20. William Frederick Cody, *An Autobiography of Buffalo Bill (Colonel W. F. Cody)* (New York: Holt, Rinehart and Company, 1920), p. 233.

21. Yost, p. 55.

22. Cody, *Autobiography*, p. 304.

23. Russell, *The Lives*, p. 190.

Chapter 5

1. William Frederick Cody, *The Life of Hon. William F. Cody Known As Buffalo Bill* (Lincoln, Nebr.: University of Nebraska Press, 1978), p. 311.

2. Joseph G. Rosa and Robin May, *Buffalo Bill and His Wild West* (Lawrence, Kans.: University Press of Kansas, 1989), p. 45.

3. Shirl Kasper, *Annie Oakley* (Norman, Okla.: University of Oklahoma Press, 1992), p. 35.

4. Don Russell, *The Lives and Legends of Buffalo Bill* (Norman, Okla.: University of Oklahoma Press, 1960), p. 199.

5. Paul O'Neil, *The End and the Myth* (Alexandria, Va.: Time-Life Books, Inc., 1979), p. 58.

6. Rosa and May, p. 46.

7. O'Neil, p. 58.

8. Ibid., p. 59.

9. Russell, p. 212.

10. Robert Paul Walker, *Great Figures of the Wild West* (New York: Facts on File, Inc., 1992), p. 35.

11. Helen Cody Wetmore, *Buffalo Bill: Last of the Great Scouts* (Chicago: The Duluth Press Publishing Company, 1899), p. 212.

12. Russell, p. 269.

13. Clyde A. Milner II, Carol A. O'Connor, and Martha A. Sandweiss, eds., *The Oxford History of the American West* (New York: Oxford University Press, 1994), p. 712.

14. Don Russell, *The Wild West* (Fort Worth, Tex.: Amon Carter Museum of Western Art, 1970), p. 39.

15. Russell, *The Lives*, p. 287.

16. Ibid.

17. Wetmore, p. 222.

18. Russell, *The Lives*, p. 254.

19. Russell, *The Wild West*, pp. 16–17.

20. Walker, p. 36.

21. Ibid.

22. Russell, *The Lives*, pp. 257–258.

23. Nellie Snyder Yost, *Buffalo Bill: His Family, Friends, Fame, Failures, and Fortunes* (Chicago: The Swallow Press, Inc., 1979), p. 99.

24. Ibid., pp. 114, 123; O'Neil, p. 78.

25. Richard Slotkin, *Gunfighter Nation: The Myth of the Frontier in Twentieth-Century America* (New York: Atheneum, 1992), p. 67.

26. Russell, *The Wild West*, p. 2.

Chapter 6

1. Richard J. Walsh and Milton S. Salsbury, *The Making of Buffalo Bill* (Indianapolis: The Bobbs-Merrill Company, 1928), p. 216.

2. Joseph G. Rosa and Robin May, *Buffalo Bill and His Wild West* (Lawrence, Kans.: University Press of Kansas, 1989), pp. 68, 70, 72.

3. Nellie Snyder Yost, *Buffalo Bill: His Family, Friends, Fame, Failures, and Fortunes* (Chicago: The Swallow Press, Inc., 1979), p. 133.

4. Rosa and May, p. 72.

5. Robert Paul Walker, *Great Figures of the Wild West* (New York: Facts on File, Inc., 1992), p. 36.

6. Rosa and May, p. 73.

7. Walsh and Salsbury, p. 229; Russell, pp. 293, 299.

8. William Frederick Cody, *Story of the Wild West and Camp-Fire Chats* (Philadelphia: Historical Publishing Company, 1888), pp. 698–699.

9. Walsh and Salsbury, p. 242.

10. Rosa and May, p. 81.

11. Don Russell, *The Wild West* (Fort Worth, Tex.: Amon Carter Museum of Western Art, 1970), p. 22.

12. Robert M. Utley, *The Lance and the Shield: The Life and Times of Sitting Bull* (New York: Henry Holt and Company, 1993), pp. 264–265.

13. Stanley Vestal, *Sitting Bull: Champion of the Sioux* (Norman, Okla.: University of Oklahoma Press, 1957), p. 251.

14. Utley, p. 265.

15. Sheila Black, *Sitting Bull and the Battle of the Little Bighorn* (Englewood Cliffs, N.J.: Silver Burdett Press, 1989), p. 114.

16. Bob Bernotas, *Sitting Bull, Chief of the Sioux* (Philadelphia: Chelsea House Publishers, 1992), p. 91.

17. Black, pp. 115–116.

18. Walter Havighurst, *Annie Oakley of the Wild West* (Lincoln, Nebr.: University of Nebraska Press, 1964), p. 93.

19. Walsh and Salsbury, pp. 260–261.

Chapter 7

1. Nellie Snyder Yost, *Buffalo Bill: His Family, Friends, Fame, Failures, and Fortunes* (Chicago: The Swallow Press, Inc., 1979), p. 184.

2. John Neihardt, *Black Elk Speaks* (Lincoln, Nebr.: University of Nebraska Press, 1979), p. 219.

3. William Frederick Cody, *Story of the Wild West and Camp-Fire Chats* (Philadelphia: Historical Publishing Company, 1888), pp. 708–711.

4. Ibid., p. 728.

5. Ibid., pp. 735–737.

6. Isabelle S. Sayers, *Annie Oakley and Buffalo Bill's Wild West* (New York: Dover Publications, Inc., 1981), p. 35.

7. Yost, p. 198.

8. Cody, pp. 742–743.

9. Joseph G. Rosa and Robin May, *Buffalo Bill and His Wild West* (Lawrence, Kans.: University Press of Kansas, 1989), p. 121.

10. Don Russell, *The Wild West* (Fort Worth, Tex.: Amon Carter Museum of Western Art, 1970), p. 18.

11. Sarah J. Blackstone, *The Business of Being Buffalo Bill: Selected Letters of William F. Cody* (New York: Praeger, 1988), p. 3.

12. Rosa and May, p. 125.

13. Yost, p. 197.

14. Glenda Riley, *The Life and Legacy of Annie Oakley* (Norman, Okla.: University of Oklahoma Press, 1994), p. 39.

15. Yost, p. 204.

16. Rosa and May, p. 135.

17. Ibid., p. 145.

18. Don Russell, *The Lives and Legends of Buffalo Bill* (Norman, Okla.: University of Oklahoma Press, 1960), p. 351.

19. Walter Havighurst, *Annie Oakley of the Wild West* (Lincoln, Nebr.: University of Nebraska Press, 1992), p. 149.

20. Mike Flanagan, *Out West* (New York: Harry N. Abrams, Inc., 1987), p. 24.

21. Russell, *The Lives*, p. 364.

22. Shirl Kasper, *Annie Oakley* (Norman, Okla.: University of Oklahoma Press, 1992), p. 123.

23. Sayers, p. 53.

24. Richard J. Walsh and Milton S. Salsbury, *The Making of Buffalo Bill* (Indianapolis: The Bobbs-Merrill Company, 1928), p. 310.

25. Yost, p. 263.

26. Russell, *The Wild West,* p. 61.

27. Russell, *The Lives,* pp. 417–418.

Chapter 8

1. Don Russell, *The Wild West* (Fort Worth, Tex.: Amon Carter Museum of Western Art, 1970), pp. 70–71.

2. Sarah J. Blackstone, *Buckskins, Bullets, and Business: A History of Buffalo Bill's Wild West* (New York: Greenwood Press, 1986), p. 63.

3. Don Russell, *The Lives and Legends of Buffalo Bill* (Norman, Okla.: University of Oklahoma Press, 1960), p. 431.

4. Nellie Snyder Yost, *Buffalo Bill: His Family, Friends, Fame, Failures, and Fortunes* (Chicago: The Swallow Press, Inc., 1979), p. 137.

5. Russell, *The Lives,* p. 421.

6. Yost, p. 327.

7. Russell, *The Lives,* p. 443.

8. Blackstone, pp. 62–63.

9. Russell, *The Lives,* pp. 448–449.

10. Joseph G. Rosa and Robin May, *Buffalo Bill and His Wild West* (Lawrence, Kans.: University Press of Kansas, 1989), pp. 182, 185, 188.

11. Shirl Kasper, *Annie Oakley* (Norman, Okla.: University of Oklahoma Press, 1992), p. 202.

12. Elizabeth Jane Leonard and Julia Cody Goodman, *Buffalo Bill: King of the Old West* (New York: Library Publishers, 1955), p. 286.

13. Buffalo Bill Memorial Museum and Grave, Lookout Mountain, Colorado, display.

14. Ibid.

Chapter 9

1. Sarah J. Blackstone, *Buckskins, Bullets, and Business: A History of Buffalo Bill's Wild West* (New York: Greenwood Press, 1986), p. 127.

2. Richard Slotkin, *Gunfighter Nation: The Myth of the Frontier in Twentieth-Century America* (New York: Atheneum, 1992), p. 67.

3. Richard White, "Frederick Jackson Turner and Buffalo Bill," in Richard White and Patricia Nelson Limerick, *The Frontier in American Culture*, ed. James R. Grossman (Berkeley, Calif.: University of California Press, 1994), p. 11.

4. Ibid., p. 29.

5. Ibid.

6. Blackstone, p. 131.

7. White, p. 27.

8. Glenda Riley, *The Life and Legacy of Annie Oakley* (Norman, Okla.: University of Oklahoma Press, 1994), p. 151.

9. William Frederick Cody, *An Autobiography of Buffalo Bill (Colonel W. F. Cody)* (New York: Holt, Rinehart and Company, 1920), p. 281.

10. Ibid.

11. Clyde A. Milner II, Carol A. O'Connor, and Martha A. Sandweiss, eds., *The Oxford History of the American West* (New York: Oxford University Press, 1994), pp. 779–780.

12. Buffalo Bill Memorial Museum and Grave, Lookout Mountain, Colorado, display.

13. Riley, pp. 158–159.

14. Blackstone, pp. 129–130.

15. Richard J. Walsh and Milton S. Salsbury, *The Making of Buffalo Bill* (Indianapolis: The Bobbs-Merrill Company, 1928), pp. 322–323.

16. Blackstone, p. 128.

17. Nellie Snyder Yost, *Buffalo Bill: His Family, Friends, Fame, Failures, and Fortunes* (Chicago: The Swallow Press, Inc., 1979), p. 413.

18. William Frederick Cody, *The Life of Hon. William F. Cody Known As Buffalo Bill* (Lincoln, Nebr.: University of Nebraska Press, 1978), p. xvi.

19. Cody, *Autobiography*, p. 3.

GLOSSARY

abolitionist—A person who wants to do away with slavery.

bankrupt—Ruined financially. When bankrupt, a person or business has more debts than assets.

bronc—An unbroken horse from western North America. It bucks, or tries to throw off its rider.

buckskin—The skin of a male deer, often used to make the clothing of frontiersmen and scouts.

czar—The ruler of Russia until the revolution in 1917.

dime novels—Low-cost paperback adventure books or magazines printed in the 1870s through 1920s. The term also referred to pulp fiction.

minstrel show—A performance of African-American songs, jokes, and culture.

mochila—The leather mailbag used by Pony Express riders.

orderly—A hospital attendant who performs routine tasks such as carrying supplies or cleaning.

pulp fiction—Sensational adventure stories printed on cheap paper. Dime novels are one example.

rodeo—An exhibition of cowboy skills such as riding and roping.

scout—A frontier guide who marked trails and led soldiers and pioneers west.

sombrero—A Spanish name for a wide-brimmed, high-crowned hat. Many of the Wild West cast wore sombreros.

vaqueros—Cowboys from Mexico.

FURTHER READING

Blackstone, Sarah J. *Buckskins, Bullets, and Business: A History of Buffalo Bill's Wild West*. New York: Greenwood Press, 1986.

Cody, William Frederick. *An Autobiography of Buffalo Bill (Colonel W. F. Cody)*. New York: Holt, Rinehart and Winston, 1920.

————. *The Life of Hon. William F. Cody Known As Buffalo Bill*. Lincoln, Nebr.: University of Nebraska Press, 1978. Reproduced from the first (1879) edition published by Frank E. Bliss, Hartford, Conn.

Rosa, Joseph G. and Robin May. *Buffalo Bill and His Wild West*. Lawrence, Kans.: University Press of Kansas, 1989.

Russell, Don. *The Lives and Legends of Buffalo Bill*. Norman, Okla.: University of Oklahoma Press, 1960.

————. *The Wild West*. Fort Worth, Tex.: Amon Carter Museum of Western Art, 1970.

Sanford, William R. and Carl R. Green. *Buffalo Bill Cody: Showman of the Wild West*. Springfield, N.J.: Enslow Publishers, Inc., 1996.

Savage, Jeff. *Scouts of the Wild West*. Springfield, N.J.: Enslow Publishers, Inc., 1995.

Walker, Robert Paul. *Great Figures of the Wild West*. New York: Facts on File, Inc., 1992.

INDEX